What's Wrong with U.S. Foreign Policy

ALSO BY C. L. SULZBERGER · *The Big Thaw*

C. L. SULZBERGER

What's Wrong with
U.S. Foreign Policy

HARCOURT, BRACE AND COMPANY

HB NEW YORK

For David, young Marina, and their generation of Americans

Acknowledgment

I wish to thank Nancy L. Ross for aid in preparing this manuscript and Marina Sulzberger and William S. Patten for assistance in improving it (although not harnessing them with any opinions expressed).

I also wish to thank Harper & Brothers for permission to quote from my book *The Big Thaw,* published in 1956.

Contents

Preface

The original kernel of this book was nourished, of all places, in Burma when, during the autumn of 1957, I was unexpectedly detained in Rangoon. It was at the time of Tazaungdaing, festival of the full moon, and merry, singing Buddhist crowds strolled through streets hung with lanterns, scattering gay firecrackers. The gold pagoda steeples were festooned with lights. Orange-robed priests, pink-robed nuns, devout men and women kneeled in front of gilt Buddhas muttering prayers while children and dogs slept before the shrines. Silver gongs boomed beneath the tinkling bell towers.

Rangoon has an oppressively sultry climate. As I sweated over a typewriter in my hotel room, immense clouds of small green insects filtered through the transom and a cumbersome air-conditioning device. Vigorous use of a Flit gun succeeded only in covering my desk and portable with a carpet of their corpses.

It is my trade to write a newspaper column three times a week, and I considered that there might be a limit to the interest of American readers in the activities of the murderous, if affable, Burmans. Therefore I began a series of articles, which I had been preparing for some while, concerning the weaknesses of United States foreign policy.

11

Later that year, in Washington, I breakfasted with Adlai Stevenson. He expressed interest in my observations and suggested I publish them in a book. At that time I had no intention of doing so. However, some months later a publisher wrote to me with a similar proposal and I decided to act upon it.

This volume, consequently, represents an extension of thoughts first expressed in an original series of six columns, thoughts again substantially repeated in the final chapter. It has been assembled, for the most part, in Aspen, Colorado, New York City, and Paris, where I live.

I hasten to say that it is not in any sense intended as an exercise in party politics. I am neither a Democrat nor a Republican. I have never voted. From the time I was first eligible to cast a presidential ballot, I have resided either in disenfranchised Washington or overseas.

It may seem to some readers that this might disqualify me, as a virtual expatriate, from expressing soundly based opinions on my own country's policy. But I protest that the laboratory where our diplomatic actions may best be observed is the world in which they are applied. And, I may add, I return to the U.S.A. with sufficient frequency to check and balance ideas conceived in other lands.

As one who has lived abroad and traveled almost continuously, I have been sadly impressed by the apparently rapid fall from our postwar position of supremacy. What are the reasons for this decline? Toynbee concludes that great empires destroy themselves. Are we, in this era of continually accelerating explosive forces, heading at a giddy pace down history's drain? If such is the case, indeed, is there not time enough to check the gravitational momentum?

I think such time remains, but only if we employ it wisely. Surely there are strong reasons for confidence in the ability and aspirations of our friends and ourselves. I agree with the words of Theodore Roosevelt: "The world has set its face hopefully toward our democracy, and, oh my fellow citizens, each one of you carries on your shoulders the burden of doing well for the sake of your own country and of seeing that the nation does well for the sake of mankind."

But for something over a decade we have not been doing well. In 1945, within the memory of anyone old enough to read this, we were the greatest nation, in terms of physical strength and in terms of an unchallenged moral position. Our escutcheon bore few tarnishes. Yet, and here I will quote a former American ambassador, William C. Bullitt: "Since the Second World War our foreign policy has led us from a pinnacle of power and security into the valley of the shadow of death."

To some degree this is, of course, the consequence of forces quite beyond our control, such as the astonishingly swift rise of Soviet Russia. But it is also the consequence of forces over which we do have control. And it is a responsibility, shared by both our major parties, whether they have been in authority or in opposition; for, in the latter case, opposition is, philosophically speaking, supposed to contribute effectively to the national interest.

It so happens that the Democrats and the Republicans have each, at the time I am writing, governed our fortunes for precisely seven years since the 1939-1945 war ended. In 1945, even after the pell-mell demobilization of our forces, the strategical position of the United States and its Western friends was good. Today it can be described at best as poor. We and our allies have forfeited bastions one by one in the Middle East and Asia. The Arabs are in arms, for the most part against us. The Chinese mainland has slipped away. We lost our brief atomic preponderance, and Soviet Russia, after an amazingly fast recovery, has become a superpower in every sense.

During this startling change in international balances, we have not, however, adjusted our basic foreign policy. We have

vacillated between fake slogans of "containment" and "liberation" from Communism, achieving neither. We have built up
in friendly but unstable countries military machines their economies cannot support. We have sought to create *status quo*
situations where none before existed and we have avoided
their creation elsewhere even when such a condition was possible. In this unsatisfactory situation we survive in nuclear
stalemate, an equilibrium of terror that cannot forever endure.

Obviously, in undertaking a book such as this, I realize
that some distinguished people with whom I claim friendship
may feel offended; but no offense is intended. As I analyze
what I feel to be the flaws in national policy, I mean no personal affront to anyone. Public figures realize, when they en-
gage to serve their country, that they become eligible for
criticism. After Lord Montgomery disagreed with General
Eisenhower in his memoirs, the President observed: "I think
I have been criticized by everybody who can write a book,
and I will be in the future." This is one of the disenchanting
features of public office. Thus, for example, I have sought to
analyze, to criticize dispassionately, the diplomacy of Secretary Dulles, despite the fact that I have been on terms of personal friendship with him for some years and despite the fact
that I have great admiration for his physical courage and in-
domitable energy, a courage and energy that have enabled
him to work with astonishing effort while overcoming illness
and fatigue.

Some readers may object along these lines: "All right, if
we are doing wrong, if our policy is failing, how would you do
things better?" I neither know nor pretend to know all the answers. Nevertheless, it is my profession, and has been for
more than twenty years, to analyze trends and facts dealing
with our diplomatic attitudes. During this period I have visited five continents and talked with hundreds of statesmen,
American and foreign. In all modesty, I attempt in these pages

to continue such analysis. The medical diagnostician is not expected to apply the surgeon's knife himself. He is summoned merely to state what, if anything, is wrong. Surely this is a respectable function. And the diagnostician of policy would be pretentious if he also boasted he could serve as surgeon.

The fact remains that I am convinced our rapid loss of power and prestige is not merely an immutable historic process. The Communists believe this; but I am not a Communist. There are factors of grave weakness in our approach to world affairs. Certainly some, if not all, of these can be corrected. My purpose is to describe these factors.

Furthermore, my approach seeks both to be unprejudiced and provocative. If I can serve in any way as gadfly, to provoke self-scrutiny, I think I shall be achieving my purpose. This purpose is not to extol the obvious positive achievements of our policy makers. These, it is blatantly evident, have been numerous.

We did, after all, take the lead in forging a coalition during World War II; we inspired the United Nations and the reconstruction of a shattered Western Europe; we have helped to restore economic well-being and some stability in large portions of the world. Such activities have been continuous under both Democratic and Republican administrations. They have met with considerable success. But, for the most part, I have refrained from discussing these positive achievements.

After all, to return to medical analogies, if one visits a doctor for diagnosis of one's gout, one is not interested to hear that teeth, hair, and heart are all in sound condition. One wishes only to learn what causes aching joints. The gout of the United States is easily to be discerned.

Chapter 1

Some Harpoon Therapy

Less than fifteen years ago we were the world's paramount power. Our reputation was unblemished. Our science, our wisdom, our principles, our generosity were renowned. We were almost in position to dictate a *Pax americana.*

What do we find today? Everywhere, or almost everywhere, we and our principles seem on the run. If, by the application of some harpoon therapy, I can help draw attention to the reasons for this trend, I shall feel content. Today, it would appear that we are in a dark wood, where the straight way is lost.

We can no longer take smug refuge in the bland assumption that our democracy must triumph because it is the best governing system yet devised by man. This assumption was perhaps correct when protected by the reality of two bands of ocean. But the oceans have shrunk.

Pericles told the citizens of another democracy: "Ours is a free state both in politics and in daily life. . . . We are superior to our enemies, too, in our preparations for war. Our city is open to the world. We are not always expelling foreigners for fear of their learning or seeing something of military importance. . . . We live freely, and yet we face the same dangers quite as readily as they. . . . Those men

17

surely should be deemed bravest who know most clearly what danger is and what pleasure is and are not made thereby to flinch." But, just a few years later, the great Athenian democracy was smashed by regimented Sparta.

This is an age of strange and revolutionary developments to which we have not yet adapted ourselves. The shibboleths of the past, which all too often satisfy us, have been outmoded, if ever they applied. Within ten years a massive great power, China, has appeared on the stage. Its importance will immutably and geometrically increase. Already in European cafés the question is posed: What is the difference between an optimist and a pessimist? The answer: An optimist learns Russian; a pessimist learns Chinese. Have we yet really faced the implications of this dynamic situation? It is time, to use Dulles's own famous words, for "an agonizing reappraisal."

Thorstein Veblen told us that "it is the frame of mind of the common man that makes the foundation of society in the modern world." Above all, this is true in a democracy such as our own. We Americans have demonstrated through our history that we are by tradition antimilitary. It is therefore perhaps paradoxical that our citizens must be persuaded each year, as is done so ably, by successive governments, that the possession of great military strength is essential if our voice is to be heard abroad and if we are to protect our heritage.

To a heavy degree our economic commitments to others have had to be expressed in terms of armed defense in order to gain legislative support. This tends to give military overtones to our foreign policy even when it is at its most defensive and most static. Besides, sending to friendly lands complex weapons, which must be maintained and repaired at a cost too great for their societies to bear, will in the end prove fruitless. And the more we invest in the armies of backward countries, the more likely we make it that they will evolve into military dictatorships.

We shall have to change the emphasis of our aid. The gap

between the have and have-not nations continues to grow not narrower but wider. High birth rates and declining death rates in the poorer countries of Africa and Asia produce a problem that can never be solved with guns. Finally, our approach has been hampered by a common misconception. Often we have wrongly assumed that nationalism everywhere may be developed into a barrier against Communist penetration. This has proved wrong and is proving wrong in Latin America, the Far and Middle East.

We have too often craved popularity and gratitude from those we seek to assist. We fail to remember that charity rarely produces genuine friendship; it is sometimes painful for others to need and receive our help.

And our domestic interests frequently influence foreign policy adversely. Congress sees to it, for example, that cutbacks in lead and zinc purchases fall mainly on overseas producers. Likewise, the requirements of Southern textile manufacturers handicap Japan's effort to sell us cloth.

The foreign-policy demands of both our political parties are shaped in terms designed to attract special blocs of voters. There is nothing particularly heinous or unusual about this fact. Indeed, such an outlook has been customary in party programs since the first platform was adopted by a National Republican Convention in 1832. As the years passed, the art of proclaiming foreign-policy objectives for internal political reasons was improved upon. After the Civil War both main parties began opposing Chinese immigration. The Democrats, with an eye on big Northern cities, went so far in 1876 as to say this "Mongolian" menace was harming "the liberty-loving German," who had by then immigrated in great masses.

In 1884 the Democrats were the first to appeal directly to a growing Irish-American electorate. They excoriated "the Republican party's British policy." Four years later they endorsed "home rule in Ireland." By 1892 the Republicans, also aware of new forces in the burgeoning population, assailed

Russian "persecution of the Jews" and supported Irish autonomy. As the technique of platform writing matured during
twelve decades, party bosses charged with editing these
pledges have been increasingly inclined to promise something
specific to almost every special-interest group. The assumption seems to be that Americans vote as minorities—not as
Americans. Fortunately, our friends abroad are learning that
as far as campaign planks on foreign affairs are concerned,
such documents primarily serve politics not policy.

Of all the questions affecting the special interests of special
segments of our population, the dreary, tormented racial
problem most acutely embarrasses our policy makers. This
issue is more important to our future during this century's
second half than any purely ideological contest. Consider the
essential paradox:

> By our own anticolonialist attitude we help accelerate the
> process by which colored races are rapidly heading toward
> a majority in global governing opinion. Yet we cannot ad-
> just our own internal relationships with those same colored
> peoples.
> With one hand we give them power in the world. With
> the other we affront them and turn their minds against us.
> The dismal consequences of such illogic are not difficult to
> forecast.

Internal politics is always reflected in our foreign politics.
The wishes of our large Jewish population cannot help being
mirrored in our relations with the predominantly Arab and
Moslem Middle East. The feelings of our many million Catholic voters are sensitive to our dealings with countries such as
Poland and Yugoslavia. The immense concern in Italy of
Americans descended from Italian immigrants is echoed in
every posture we assume toward the land from which they
originated. But each of these special groups, however, must
remember the priority of our nation's over-all interests.

At this critical epoch we seem to have developed an odd contempt for the human brain just at a moment when that organ should be most hallowed. Our educational system was permitted to run down. The sneering term of "egghead" was invented for those above the mental norm. The intellectual in the United States has, occasionally, almost had to pretend to be a boob in order to gain respect. At our greatest periods the egghead was a venerated individual, a man like Franklin, Jefferson, or Theodore Roosevelt. But today's locker-room civilization too often either scoffs at or ignores him.

We have become overly concerned with how we sell things rather than with what we sell. When the combustion engine doomed a heavily capitalized horse-feed industry, we sold ourselves the habit of eating bran for breakfast. Today we sell democracy to nations like South Vietnam or Pakistan—with little concern as to whether theirs is a proper ideological market.

The best advertising techniques can neither gild mediocrity nor advance unsuitable causes. The advertising expert has a profound influence upon our phase of civilization. He is our special contribution, the great and original American technician, as indigenous and peculiar to us as, in other corners of the world, the Malayan fish-listener or the Soviet political commissar to a track team. But advertising must analyze its markets. Foreign policy, because it is designed to improve our world position, must be aimed at foreigners and not ourselves. It is not, as some of our citizens occasionally seem to think, a concession to other lands that we even have a foreign policy; it is indispensable to our survival.

In conceiving a foreign policy we must be sure always to seek proper objectives and those that, within practical possibility, appear attainable. It is not essential always to strive for action. In foreign policy it is better nine times out of ten to sit still than to do the brilliant thing.

The style of its application, furthermore, is all-important.

As Lord Chesterfield wrote: "Style is the dress of thoughts." A right policy, wrongfully presented, can suffer. This is a factor we have all too often ignored. Our ebulliently energetic Secretary of State has come to be associated in many minds abroad with activities and prejudices that do not truly represent our intentions.

In 1958 an English weekly staged a competition. It awarded prizes for the best description of "mechanical marvels," among which was listed a "Foster." One definition submitted was: "FOSTER: Fear of Soviet Territorial Expansion Reactor: The reactor responds vigorously to an intake of assorted rumor-flashes, and polarizes them (with the built-in PPF or prejudice polarizing factor) to a steady anti-red beam. Functions best when completely in the dark and facing East. Emits occasional loud clangs when operating: these, though disturbing, should be ignored."

Another read: "FOSTER: Fulcrometer of Stability and True Equilibrium Restorer: This is a meter for cliff-edge naturalists, etc., showing how far it is safe to lean over the edge without actually toppling over. Fractional margins are clearly indicated and just before C.C. (Certain Calamity) point is reached the Equilibrium Restorer comes automatically into action balancing the wearer back into safety. An Indispensable instrument for those indulging in Brinkmanship. 'Keeps your grip on terror firmer.' "

How much do we deceive ourselves when we assume, by the very labels we apply, that we speak truly for a free world? What we mean by this expression is, of course, the area beyond the Iron Curtain. This area includes seventy-two countries. But forty-nine of them are governed either by dictatorships or oligarchies, by no means all benevolent. Several operate under systems of economic feudalism.

And how about ourselves? Should we not ponder some of our own shortcomings as viewed by other peoples: inadequate education, racial discrimination, religious bigotry, political and economic smugness, juvenile delinquency, antiquated public health, outdated prisons and mental institutions, a shortage of doctors and medical facilities, insufficient funds for scientific research? In order to revitalize our foreign policy, is it not also requisite to revitalize our own society? Can we present to others the picture of vibrant leadership if we permit our own concepts to remain jaded?

As a reader can see, I am deliberately seeking the provocative approach to these problems. Let us recall the picture of America that for so long existed in the imagination abroad: a haven of opportunity for the oppressed, a land of golden chance for all, regardless of birthplace. Who believes this now? Thousands and thousands of immigrants came to our shores for two and a half centuries: oppressed English, French, Irish, Scandinavians, Russians, Hungarians, Italians; Jews, Catholics, Protestants. The pressure for admission has shifted to the overpopulated colored lands of Africa and Asia. Yet we do not admit many of their citizens.

This fact is directly related to the most important moral issue facing us—and we ourselves have insisted upon the morality of our attitudes. That issue is racial integration— on a basis of full freedom and equality. I repeat that we cannot hope to assert world leadership unless we resolve this tragic and perplexing question. Asia and Africa have become key continents, whose future political sympathies will fix the international balance. Yet every time their multitudinous peoples are reminded that we, in the professed land of liberty, still treat many Negroes as second-class citizens, our prestige diminishes.

It is extraordinary how this fundamental heartache, which helped foster the original Republican party, has remained at the core of American politics for more than a century while the country grew from lusty immaturity to superpower. In 1858 Lincoln described the problem in words that even today find echoes from India to the Gold Coast. He said: "Our reliance is in the love of liberty which God has planted in our bosoms. Our defense is in the preservation of the spirit which prizes liberty as the heritage of *all men, in all lands everywhere.* Destroy this spirit and you have planted the seeds of despotism around your own doors."

Two years later, the Supreme Court's attitude became politically important in the argument on Negro slavery. The Northern Democratic faction (in a split party) used judicial decisions on private property to defend an equivocal position. Its platform advised the electorate: "The Democratic party will abide by the decisions of the Supreme Court of the United States on the questions of Constitutional law."

Does this remind one hauntingly of recent arguments? Even today, some Southern Democrats, staunchly defending an outmoded cause, speak in a fashion that provoked Republicans in 1876 to use words strikingly familiar for other and shocking reasons. Their platform then said: "We charge the Democratic party with being the same in character and spirit as when it *sympathized with treason.*"

Former Governor George B. Timmerman of South Carolina, a world traveler who apparently wears blinkers, still argues that integration of our armed forces, by sending Negro troops abroad, "is building deep-seated hatred for the United States." "India," says he, "isn't interested in the Negro—or the white man. It is ridiculous to think these people worry about what Americans do." He considers that desegregation in District of Columbia schools "is not a good advertisement of democracy to foreign diplomats" and recommends that envoys from "colored" nations should, when traveling in the South, stay in the "best available *nigra* hotels."

This kind of bigotry does the United States more harm in a world that has evolved somewhat more than South Carolina than can be remedied by any number of exquisite speeches pronounced in public forums by our statesmen. There is no easy answer to the question. Neither sensible Democrats nor

Republicans of any race wish to fan conflicts in our troubled land. Courage and self-sacrifice on the part of our national leaders are constantly required. They must say to the American people, and to the point of redundancy, that we cannot aspire to any position of moral leadership unless we can succeed in giving a happy place in our own life to the colored people here.

When one regards the violent history of nationalism and racism in the rest of the world, one must be thankful for the astonishing gentleness and good humor of the Negroes in the United States. It is our fortune that they neither showed the traits of sullen Peruvian Indians nor banded together in armed outrage like the Palestinian Stern gang or Cypriot E.O.K.A. All Communism's concentrated power never attracted from their ranks more than a handful of "intelligentsia." But these people do not yet feel, as a race, admitted to equal citizenship, although asked to make the ultimate contribution of joining our armed forces. The question should not be rushed to the point of provoking trouble or frightening the South. But white Americans must constantly remind themselves that the bulk of this world's population is colored differently. We cannot pretend to be a valid model for democracy if we continue, even regionally, to insist on race superiority. Moreover, we must never close too tightly the gates of immigration, through which our country's vigor is renewed. Refreshing the national bloodstream has been a factor in our history. Much intellectual stimulus in the Central and Northern states derived from successive waves of Germans, Poles, and Scandinavians. Between the two world wars our entry laws began to restrict this beneficial flow; but Axis persecution brought to these shores some of the best of Europe's brains.

Sociologists might be tempted to see a connection between the regional growth of mental provincialism and the dwindling of new immigration. The nation's cultural product as a whole has not diminished. But in widespread areas there has been an increasing tendency toward separation of the cultural from the anticultural.

The eggheads—so defined with inferred distaste—draw toward centers of specific mental gravity—large cities and universities. There, first-rate intellectual communities flourish. Nevertheless, as a result of polarization, the intervening interior suffers impoverishment. It is like France, where Paris's magnetic attraction drains off the best talent. Fallow, between these poles, lie areas of the commonplace, satisfied with the limited stimulus of mass-produced cinematic and journalistic media.

Our traditions in both the recent and the distant past have been animated by the energies and ideas of immigrants. Surely this nation, with its craving to increase an already astonishing productivity, can easily absorb new citizens from stifled portions of the world. Due reflection confirms the value of this custom. In 1956, in Budapest, the dictator of Communist Hungary asked me: "Do you know how many of our people know the secret of the atom bomb?" He numbered off a list: Leo Szilard, John von Neumann, Edward Teller, Eugen Wigner. All had become United States citizens. And it is extraordinary how swiftly new arrivals in our country are in every sense acclimatized. The strongest single force impelling immigrants is the desire to be accepted as Americans.

Indeed, this has caused the political analyst Samuel Lubell to observe: "Because of our heritage of immigration most of us are also under some compulsion to demonstrate that we are more American than other Americans. It would almost seem that the more painful the frustrations endured by any immigrant group in its efforts to be Americanized, the more violent is its recoil of patriotism."

In any democracy, as I have pointed out, there is an acutely intimate relationship between internal and external affairs. It has been said: "Foreign politics demand scarcely any of those qualities which are peculiar to a democracy; they require, on the contrary, the perfect use of almost all those in which it is deficient." This observation was published in 1835 by Alexis de Tocqueville in his prescient study of *Democracy in America*. Tocqueville was sympathetic to the aspirations of this then-new system of government, but he found it ill-suited to diplomacy. "A democracy," he wrote, "can only with great difficulty regulate the details of an important undertaking, persevere in a fixed design, and work out its execution in spite of serious obstacles. It cannot combine its measures with secrecy or await their consequences with patience." He concluded: "Almost all the defects inherent in democratic institutions are brought to light in the conduct of foreign affairs; their advantages are less perceptible." He doubted "what degree of sagacity the American democracy will display in the conduct of the foreign policy of the country."

These remarks remain applicable today. Both the admirers and detractors of our statesmen should contemplate them as we face arduous tasks. Apart from any administration's proficiencies or deficiencies, the following circumstances must always be taken into account:

The secretary of state, working with the president, must act by the device of executive agreement to move swiftly in a diplomatic sense to keep this country abreast of its role in a turbulent world.

The nation as a whole seems prepared to accept with little complaint and less understanding the evolution of our attitudes in vital areas that increasingly commit us under growing difficulties.

A vociferous but uninfluential minority of "intellectuals" worries about this trend. It rebukes the administration not only for its decisions but for the very means of taking such decisions. Yet this has little practical impact.

The opposition party in Congress frequently complains of our diplomacy as practiced, whether by Acheson or Dulles.

But there are few positive suggestions for radical change in the method of making policy.

Indeed, legislators from both parties have abdicated. They do not accept sufficient responsibility by helping to shape our attitudes through public pronouncements or private counsel.

We are left in a position where our practice of foreign affairs is excoriated by Congressmen of each party, for differing reasons, while the public remains indifferent.

Some Republican senators of the more conservative and less-informed ilk denounce the President and Secretary Dulles for not doing enough to counteract the global growth of Communist influence. Meanwhile, some Democratic senators arrive at similar conclusions from a totally different angle. But neither faction can persuade its party to agree on delineating an alternative.

The Democrats today have no effective role as an opposition voice in diplomacy. Indeed, their influence has less echo upon our policy, as shown during the 1958 Middle Eastern crisis, than that of the British Labor party; for Her Majesty's Loyal Opposition can galvanize public support behind its own coherent program, forcing the Conservative Government to modify its stand and thereby influencing American pronouncements.

Senators who criticize Dulles, with justification, for some of his actions might criticize themselves with equal justification for permitting him to take such actions, for whether the Secretary of State is right or wrong in his judgments, he is almost forced by our system to make and apply such judgments.

Tocqueville wrote: "We have seen that the Federal Constitution entrusts the permanent direction of the external interests of the nation to the President [which means also the secretary of state] and the Senate." But, by its habit of signing predated blank checks like the Eisenhower Doctrine, the

Senate is abdicating its prerogatives. The formulation of policy is being thrust more and more into the hands of the executive, with less and less of a senatorial corrective power. Such tendencies are encouraged by the pressure of a world quite different from that which existed when our Constitution was drafted. But critics might well ponder the system that permits mistakes to occur with a minimum of effective criticism.

From Truman's administration on, there has been a steadily increasing tendency by our executive branch to involve us in a condition of war (as in Korea) or to risk involving us in such a condition (as in Lebanon) without prior legislative approval. Likewise, the president, without much comment or objection, can now virtually obligate the nation in treaty commitments such as the Baghdad Pact minus the formality of Senate ratification.

This practice, wisely applied, seems to be acknowledged by both parties as a necessity during these days of instant dangers in a world where our strategic interests are widespread. Thus, even Democratic senators who have been critical of present Middle Eastern policies do not, on the whole, question the necessity for swift executive action. However, our policy is perhaps changing by maturation. We gradually approach a situation where there is danger that such swift executive action might involve us in disputes not germane to our true national interests. This is especially possible when we contemplate frustrating indirect aggression.

Hitherto, our announced intention has been to commit ourselves against all aggression in which the hand of "international Communism" may be detected as a guiding force. But in Lebanon we already had to modify such concepts in 1958. Subversion there was expressed in direct and indirect aid by Egypt's Nasser to the rebels. Yet Nasser then had his own leading Communists locked up. Thus, policy, as applied in Lebanon, seemed to omit the usual Communist label.

We wish to frustrate oblique aggressive menaces through

the U.N. But it is hard to define subversive propaganda or, in areas of shifting populations, to prove infiltration. For example, thousands of armed nomads, some of whom check their guns at the border and some of whom do not, annually drift across the Afghanistan-Pakistan frontier.

Obviously, we cannot afford to underwrite all existing governments against the political forces that might upset them. This would even commit us to protecting the East European satellite regimes against our own propaganda and against help for popular uprisings.

We often assume that the most effective brake on erroneous policy of government is exercised by public opinion. Jefferson believed that "whenever the people are well-informed they can be trusted with their own government." A question that seemingly lies at the heart of this is: How well informed are the American people?

When the Eisenhower administration decided to ban a projected visit to Communist China by American newspapermen, it claimed to be acting "in the best interests of the United States." The wisdom of this judgment has yet to be proved. Presumably Peiping knew, in extending its original invitation, that Washington, if it approved the journey, would be politically embarrassed with a considerable and emotional body of our public. On the other hand, the Chinese must have assumed we might be diplomatically embarrassed in Asia if the journey were not approved. But our attitude made us appear unnecessarily foolish. The press in such free Asian countries as Thailand and Burma criticized our government for hypocrisy.

The Republican platform said in 1956: "We will overlook no opportunity that, with prudence, can be taken to bring about a progressive elimination of the barriers that interfere with the free flow of news, information and ideas." Was the administration's negative decision prudent? Is it wise to spurn an opportunity to learn at first hand and from reliable sources something about a massive country with which we verge on open war? Is it sounder to depend upon foreign sources? Should our government presume to suspect that our journalists might be duped? Is it a proper State Department function to censor our press by indirect means through limiting access to news areas?

These are grave questions and they do not appear to have been adequately answered. Nor does one easily find a precedent for the administration's attitude. The State Department threatened penal action against persons violating its ukase. On what ground? Although we did not recognize the Soviet Union until 1933, leading American news agencies and papers had correspondents there for years before. At least one American reporter traveled through Communist Albania when we had no relations with that country. Nothing was said. Correspondents have visited Bulgaria, North Vietnam, and Outer Mongolia, none of which we recognize. Senator George W. Malone went to Bulgaria on an ordinary passport. He was neither criticized nor prosecuted. There is a difference in degree between these Communist lands and China. American hostages are still held by Peiping. But it is difficult to argue that they will be more easily extricated simply by refusing to allow newspapermen to report on their situation.

The China ban underscores the illogical history of our relationships with foreign countries. We are not yet even sure what diplomatic recognition implies. But we tend increasingly to use it as a mild indication of approval. Surely we do not approve of governments in the U.S.S.R. or the satellites. We do not care for several little despotisms in Central America. We never liked Argentina's Peron—but we recognized him. Our general attitude to the world around us remains somewhat confusing. What is the logic in continuing to recognize Lithuania, Esthonia, and Latvia, dispossessed twenty years ago? There is no rival government to that in Communist Albania—but we must refuse relations. We do not recognize Outer Mongolia, but seem prepared to accept it into the U.N., and our journalists travel there. And, curiously, while we deal with the Vatican, we have not exactly recognized it.

Another confusion is on the subject of political "interference." We have never tolerated interference by other nations in our own internal affairs, and our citizens boast with proper righteousness that we do not aspire to interfere in the affairs of others. But this is simply not the truth. We interfered up to our elbows to assure a government in Greece upon which we could look with favor. We interfered in France, during the late nineteen forties, to succor a Third Force coalition and prevent Charles de Gaulle's first effort to return to power. During the 1948 Italian elections we grossly interfered; our ambassador toured Italy making speeches deliberately calculated to sway voters. These actions are not always improper. They are prompted by a duty imposed upon us by two factors: we are a superpower and charged with protection of our friends; and we are opposed by a clever system seeking to exploit the democratic processes to undermine those same friends. Let us face this and acknowledge it.

As a matter of fact, there has been remarkable continuity under both Democrats and Republicans in approaching this essential matter. There is *no* philosophical difference in the aims of what have been called the Truman, Eisenhower, and Dulles "doctrines." On March 12, 1949, Truman told Congress: "It must be the policy of the United States to support free peoples who are resisting attempted subjugation by armed minorities or by outside pressures." The broad purpose of the Truman Doctrine was to assert a claim to the right to intervene even when there was no intention to exercise this right completely. Likewise, these are the asserted purposes of the Eisenhower and Dulles doctrines. They were implicit in the Monroe Doctrine.

Apart from direct intervention in the fate of other nations

and apart from the development of an overextended network of purely military pacts where, as Shelley would have said, "Our calculations have outrun conception; we have eaten more than we can digest," we have developed, as is proper for a rich, capitalistic state, an economic approach to the task of securing other peoples' freedom. The belief that American private wealth should play an influential part in bettering life in foreign lands is not new. Religious missions, private relief agencies, and charitable foundations had long worked abroad. What is more recent is the development of the theory and practice of using government funds for such purposes and to improve our foreign-policy position. And the size of these public efforts has come to dwarf the relative extent of private efforts. Many Democrats and such Republican liberals as Douglas Dillon and James H. Smith, Jr., have come to realize that economic expansion is now a first political priority in the free world. It is an essential both in terms of shoring up weak lands against Communism and in terms of insuring the health of our extensive international commerce.

This economic approach to diplomacy is one of the most important developments of postwar foreign policy. The other novel factor, which links peacetime aid with military defense, is the intrusion upon diplomacy of nuclear science. On the one hand, we have begun to face the immense challenge of aiding poor nations by helping them to produce power from previously unknown sources. On the other hand, both in our strategic calculations and in our efforts for world disarmament, we are forced to consider the implications of the atom.

In this respect, we lagged too long in pressing for a freeze on weapons testing. This was disadvantageous from a propaganda viewpoint. It was probably also disadvantageous from a military point of view. An enforced, early suspension of testing by all nuclear nations might leave us in our present position of relative technological superiority in explosive warheads as distinct from missiles. And we would be more likely to retain this advantage under a freeze than by continued tests. If experiments continue, the Russians are quite as likely as we to discover some radically new innovation.

I have briefly touched on a number of subjects many of which will be dealt with more intensively in following chapters. At the risk of repetition I would like to stress certain points.

The time has come for new self-scrutiny, a re-examination not only of the style and methods of our policy but the objectives to which it aspires. And no such scrutiny can take place unless we assume a more humble position regarding ourselves, our nation, and our faults. We must abandon a tendency to moral hectoring of others and an addiction to apocalyptic slogans designed, at best, to appeal to our voters. These frighten our friends at least as much as our enemies.

The coming decade is one in which we shall have to focus our diplomatic attentions far more closely on Africa and Asia than on relatively stable Europe. In the West our policy, as expressed through the Marshall Plan and NATO, has met with unquestionable success. But should our diplomacy take all the credit? History, we must remember, works with us in this area. Wherever Communism spreads into the Occident it tends, on the whole, to bring with it a lower standard of living and a philosophy abhorrent to the peoples living there. However, where Communism spreads southward and eastward from Russia, it tends to bring with it a higher standard of living and often an improvement over previous governing philosophies. We must not ignore this truism when we set about rectifying a Middle East policy that has been absurd and a Far East policy that has been lamentable.

I am not a defeatist. I do not believe in Lord Russell's supine preference for Soviet domination rather than, if it is required, a desperate nuclear defense. But we must reform and vitalize both ourselves and that foreign policy which expresses our intentions to the world. This requires daring—including the daring to admit and correct mistakes. The alternative is timidity. And the ultimate fate of timidity is failure.

Thomas Jefferson wrote: "Timid men prefer the calm of despotism to the boisterous sea of liberty."

Chapter 2

How Our Policy Is Administered

Constitutionally, the president of the United States is responsible for conducting foreign policy. Congress has the right to approve or reject treaties, to declare war, to provide the funds without which our diplomacy would be helpless, and to veto appointment of envoys. But the executive power of the White House is paramount in relationships abroad.

This responsibility was most recently defined in 1936 by a Supreme Court opinion of Justice George Sutherland (*U.S. v. Curtiss-Wright Export Corporation*); "He [the president] alone negotiates. Into the field of negotiation the Senate cannot intrude; the Congress is powerless to invade it."

The foreign-policy role of the chief executive has become ever more important as the relative world authority of the United States increased. Indeed, it is perhaps not too much to say that nowadays this is his most important role. Our country can no longer pretend to the simple isolationist creed of the Founding Fathers. Involved in pacts with more than half the world's nations and in complex international trade and financial commitments, we can scarcely imagine today that Jeffersonian doctrine: "Commerce with all nations, alliance with none."

Since the days of Woodrow Wilson, presidents have chosen two means of applying this developing authority. Some have

36

tended to keep the diplomatic reins in their own hands by often ignoring the traditional machinery established to govern relationships abroad. Thus Woodrow Wilson relied heavily on Colonel E. M. House, and Franklin D. Roosevelt relied even more heavily on Harry Hopkins or on Sumner Welles, a diplomatic official but never secretary of state. Eisenhower, as will be explained later, has in a sense been allowed by circumstance to avoid such a choice, for his Secretary of State has managed by constant travel to combine in his own person that office's functions with those of special presidential agent.

The position of secretary of state is becoming increasingly unpopular in American eyes. Indeed, since the United States became a superpower, there has been a tendency to criticize any man who held this office. Algebraically, one might say, the popularity of our principal diplomatic agent has been almost inversely proportional to the extent of his responsibilities. This public attitude encourages the habit of denouncing the president's foreign minister personally for partly political reasons. Such was certainly the case with Dean Acheson. And it is at least equally the case with Dulles. The Republicans, although many knew better, cast unfair brickbats at Acheson and grossly exaggerated his responsibility for events abroad that were quite beyond his control. The Democrats tended to apply the same formula to Dulles. The office of secretary of state is, by its very nature, bound to be unpopular. If a secretary is to be successful today, he must recognize the need to serve as a whipping boy.

The presidency, nationally regarded as the most important post in the world, carries with it a certain nimbus of glory. Between elections there is a tendency to place a halo on the president's head, as far as the outer world is concerned. But the secretary of state has no such aura of untouchability. According to James F. Byrnes, who held the office from 1945 to 1947, this is as it should be. Byrnes served in all three governmental branches: judicial (as Supreme Court justice), legislative (as representative and senator), and executive (as wartime mobilization director, secretary of state, and governor). When once I discussed the subject with him in Columbia, South Carolina, he said: "One of the functions of a good secretary of state is to be unpopular," for, as Byrnes pointed out, in external relationships that official must represent policies that are disliked by some other nations, since they are drafted in our own interest. And, in internal relationships, the secretary is bound to offend one or another of the disparate economic, regional, emotional, religious, or other groups that make up this curiously cosmopolitan land. Byrnes added: "He must be strong enough to resist demands from factions within the country having at heart some particular or local grievance. It is proper that such particularized views and pressures should be expressed. That is the way our democracy works. There is no way of preventing this; nor should there be. But, at the same time, the secretary of state must be strong enough to say no. And this will make him unpopular."

There is in our heritage a habit of mistrusting foreign governments and those we name to deal with them. Furthermore, it is political custom to hold the unfortunate State Department responsible for disliked actions of those governments which it is supposed to bend to our will. Acheson suffered most unfairly on this account. One of the merriest Republican occupations has been to hold Truman's Secretary personally responsible for China's collapse, the invasion of South Korea, and the extension of Soviet power into Eastern Europe. And the Democrats are getting their own back with a vengeance. Dulles came to symbolize for them the fall of Dienbienphu, the growth of Arab nationalism, and the rise in world prestige of the Sino-Soviet bloc.

There is perhaps a skeleton of justice in both attitudes. As for the flesh of the argument, we must learn to recognize that despite our great tangible power there exist forces we cannot dominate.

Both Acheson and Dulles are exceedingly intelligent men. Acheson was much admired overseas for the clarity of his arguments. But the fact that his personality was so well received abroad perhaps incited irritation in this country, which still retains a strong stamp of psychological isolationism. Dulles, aware of this handicap in his predecessor, leaned over backward to get on with Congress. But he inclined toward the most intellectually barren elements of Congress. And he inclined so far that many of our friends—above all, Britain and France—became distressed. Frequently, a Dulles statement designed to placate legislators unloosed torrents of foreign irritation.

One would have to be either partisan or fool to regard the Eisenhower administration's Middle Eastern policy as successful. And certainly the Democrats, who first aided Tito and contained the Russians at Berlin, deserve much credit for any later successes in East Europe. However, the record of the Roosevelt and Truman administrations in the Orient also left much to be desired. But to say that in either instance the State Department alone was responsible for destiny's whirlwinds is mere politicking.

It is an odd circumstance that with more and more frequency we choose our secretaries of state from the legal profession. With the exception of Edward R. Stettinius and George C. Marshall, every secretary since 1933 came from the ranks of the law. As commentary on this habit, there is a shrewd opinion, conceived more than two centuries ago, in *De la manière de négocier avec les souverains,* possibly the most valuable treatise on diplomatic methods. Published in Paris in 1713, it was written by François de Callières, the private secretary of King Louis XIV and an ambassador in the French diplomatic service. Even at that early date, Callières was constrained to write: "In general, the training of a lawyer breeds habits and dispositions of mind which are not favorable to the practice of diplomacy." The implication is simple.

A lawyer is more interested in winning a case than in developing a long-range program; he is likely to be more facile than wise; he may be more concerned with exploiting flaws in an opponent's argument than in attaining reasonable and enduring solutions. Furthermore, a lawyer is used to changing positions with remarkable adroitness.

I think it is fair to say that Secretary Dulles has displayed all of these tendencies. Beyond doubt a brilliant negotiator at the conference table, he has, nevertheless, depended heavily upon this ability to extricate himself and us as best as possible from crises that might have proved unnecessary with more careful advance planning.

Two other cautionary phrases of Callières are worth notice. Negotiators, he wrote, "must possess the patience of a watchmaker and be devoid of personal prejudice." (To which one might append the counsel of Sir Anthony Eden, a far better diplomatist than he was a prime minister: "Hurried diplomacy, believe me, is usually bad diplomacy.") And Callières also wrote: "Menaces always do harm to negotiation, since they often push a party to extremes to which they would not have resorted but for provocation."

It would be inaccurate to describe Dulles as a man "devoid of personal prejudices," and his frenetic global voyages sometimes smack so much of "hurried diplomacy" that one feels impelled to inquire whether perpetual motion can be a substitute for foreign policy. Finally, the employment of "menaces" is one of his favorite tactics; he has exploited it in his famous "brink of war" theory and in acerb statements to our friends, such as his "agonizing reappraisal" warning to the French that they had better mend their ways.

Dulles is a man capable both of changing his mind with dazzling speed and of employing skillful legal tactics to obscure the fact that he has not in reality shifted his position. This may be gathered from the following incident. In early May 1952, when Dulles first discussed with General Eisenhower (then still NATO commander) the possibility of becoming his secretary of state, his ideas on policy were somewhat different from those of the future president. In Europe, Dulles felt, the United States erred in placing West German integration into the North Atlantic community ahead of Germany's unification. But by then Eisenhower vigorously supported the European Defense Community.

Furthermore, Dulles was skeptical about Eisenhower's views on Asia. Dulles had spent months working on a Japanese peace treaty for the Truman administration. He felt there was a tendency to subordinate our interests in the Orient to our interests in Europe. He had already discussed this matter with Admiral Arthur W. Radford, then Pacific naval commander. Radford and Dulles agreed that American strategy should be founded on the theory that potential aggressors must be warned that if they broke the peace we would not necessarily move against them at the point of aggression; we would hit back where and when we desired. Finally, as a result of the Korean war, which then dominated political thinking, they advocated that, if possible, United States troops should never again be employed on the Asian mainland.

Eisenhower, by eventually appointing Dulles and Radford to key positions, appeared to accept these ideas. However, he was continually on the alert lest such concepts give the appearance that we were abandoning Europe and relying for our defense solely upon retaliatory striking air power and Herbert Hoover's "fortress America" concept.

The Republican Convention that nominated Eisenhower for president met in Chicago Monday, July 7, 1952. The day before it started I dropped in to see General Lucius Clay, an important behind-the-scenes figure in the Eisenhower faction, at his suite in the Blackstone Hotel. Clay was very disturbed by the use of the words "retaliatory striking power" in the national-defense plank of the proposed platform. He thought this implied that a Republican administration would rely solely on long-range strategic atomic bombing, or, in other words, the "fortress America" theory.

The defense plank, as initially drafted, read: "On the prudent assumption that Communist Russia may not accommodate our own disgraceful lagging preparedness, we should develop with utmost speed a force in being, as distinguished from paper plans, of such *retaliatory striking* power as to deter sudden attack or promptly and decisively defeat it."

Later that same Sunday, I lunched with Eisenhower, two of his brothers, Milton and Earl, and Senator Frank Carlson. I asked the General what he thought of the platform draft. He replied that he had not seen the actual text but that Dulles, the previous evening, had given him a verbal outline. I inquired: "What did you think of the defense plank, specifically the reference to retaliation?"

"Do they use that word?" he asked. "I simply won't accept it. Not only won't I take that on the platform, I would rather not run than accept it."

Eisenhower considered this a vital issue and was most disturbed. When he is upset he has a habit of walking up and down and his color rises. He put aside his luncheon plate (we were eating off our laps in his sitting room) and strode about angrily.

That evening I had a drink with Dulles and his wife. He asked how I had found the General. "Irked," I replied and told him why. Dulles seemed surprised. "Does that phrase still bother him?" asked its author. (Dulles, although charged only with supervising preparation of the foreign-policy plank, had been able to get his pet theory adopted in the defense section.) "Maybe I can do something about it."

Two days later I again had a drink with Dulles. "Everything's okay now," he said. I inquired how he had removed the offending words. He answered: "Oh, I went to see Millikin and got him to take them out." (Senator Eugene D. Millikin was chairman of the platform-drafting or resolutions committee.) "He was too dumb to understand their significance."

This is what I would call a "legalistic" approach. The same Dulles who had seen to it that the offending words were incorporated in the platform draft saw to it that they were removed. In this instance it is clear that he did not change his opinions; only their appearance. During the 1952 presidential campaign both the words and the theory crept back into Dulles's public statements. And they became the heart of his famous "brink of war" approach as secretary of state.

Dulles is a remarkable man, with great physical courage and endurance and a direct, simple manner that can be charming in small company. He is also unabashedly ambitious. From the time of his youth, he interested himself in foreign affairs, and both his grandfather John Foster and his uncle Robert Lansing were secretaries of state. For several years he had carefully prepared himself for that role, both through personal study and travel and through shrewd political connections.

Shortly before the 1948 presidential election, when it seemed sure the Republican candidate, Thomas E. Dewey, would win, I lunched with Dulles in Paris and asked him if it was a certainty, in that event, that he would be Dewey's secretary. Dulles replied, to my astonishment, that he had not yet made up his mind. He wondered if it would not be more interesting to have a special job as roving presidential agent, "like Colonel House or Harry Hopkins." With brilliant ingenuity he later combined the two assignments under Eisenhower.

The loyalty between Eisenhower and Dulles has proved to be, in many respects, remarkably similar to that which existed between Truman and Acheson. The President undoubtedly considered Dulles particularly effective despite not infrequent criticism both here and abroad.

By May 1952 he was Eisenhower's choice to head the State Department—two months before the nomination and six months before the voting. However, Dulles was not yet entirely positive that he wished the post he had coveted so long. He used to reflect that in this modern age it might be more stimulating and perhaps more useful to play a less formally restricted role. To resolve this evident dichotomy of aspiration, Dulles became not only Eisenhower's secretary of state, but also his principal traveling diplomatist. This novel approach stimulated praise from admirers and criticism from detractors.

The admirers contend that Dulles familiarized himself with world affairs and statesmen by his constant flying voyages. They maintain that he brought to bear Washington's full influence during delicate negotiations and at crucial moments by speaking directly, without need for cumbersome, traditional exchanges through ambassadorial channels. The detractors take a wholly opposite view. They argue that Dulles was absent from Washington so much that efforts to elaborate long-range policy consequently suffered; that he was rarely available when foreign diplomats wished to discuss their urgent problems with him. As a result, they assert, there were often lapses in effective interchange between such envoys and our government, because, under existing administrative organization, power has become too diffuse. Finally, they insist that the status of our own ambassadors abroad was lowered by the frequency of Dulles's travels; that the Secretary's direct diplomacy caused regular channels of contact to dry up.

Both views are defended with logic and vehemence. But there can be no doubt about one point: the role of the secretary of state has changed. Dulles modified and agitated the more restrained techniques of Acheson. The Constitution envisioned a senior Cabinet member with predominant influence in diplomatic policy. This job has developed into that of executive assistant in foreign affairs, for which the president retains basic responsibility. There have been instances (notably House and Hopkins) when the White House modified this relationship by intruding special appointees. Dulles precluded such a possibility by serving both as secretary and presidential envoy.

Coincidental with this new approach, however, the administrative domain of foreign affairs continued to expand. Indeed, eventually it may be desirable to concentrate in one office all subordinate responsibilities for our overseas interests.

This might mean strengthening the position of secretary of state and placing under it the control not only of diplomacy but also of military relationships abroad, trade, economic aid, propaganda. Or a new office could be created, perhaps a presidential deputy of Cabinet rank, to supervise these related functions.

The growing ramifications of our world interests are not yet so neatly ordered as other administrative aspects of the presidency. Dulles avoided the disparate tendencies of a Roosevelt-Hull-Hopkins-Welles relationship. But with the development of new foreign-policy problems and with his tireless traveling, a system of self-paralysis crept in. Many among our own envoys are dissatisfied. They feel that too often while Dulles was away their cabled reports were read by officials of insufficient stature. In Washington there sometimes is a feeling of frustration among both foreign diplomats and American officials anxious to clarify vital policy matters. There is a sense of not being able to manipulate urgent problems through a labyrinth of overlapping agencies. And when the United States cannot act swiftly enough, reality passes us by.

Perhaps, rather than combine the functions of secretary of state and traveling presidential agent, it might be wiser to unite all foreign-affairs functions into the former's portfolio—and keep him more at home. Such is the implication of a pleasant legend: Eisenhower summons Dulles to him, saying: "Foster, don't just do something—stand there."

The injection of traveling-salesman techniques into the functions of secretary of state was not the only change in

Dulles's approach to the office. With a curious hint of psychological insecurity, he stressed the need for "positive loyalty" to himself by his staff. And he allowed his desires for simonpure security in the national interest to develop into a disgusting witch hunt among the members of our diplomatic service. These two developments combined to lower both the efficiency and morale of an important governmental arm.

Dulles, who possesses a fine mind, has immense confidence in his own ability to solve the pressing problems of our time. He tended in office to rely far less than his predecessors upon expert counsel or provocative disagreement among his advisers. In fact, with the blazing exception of Douglas Dillon, he sought competent but agreeable yes men as his intimate associates. He reduced the functions of the Policy Planning Staff, which was supposed to plan for future contingencies. This body did not even have a position paper drafted for the likely event that Egypt might assume control of the all-important Suez Canal.

Furthermore, because of the cumbersome security program Dulles instituted, the United States gradually lost prestige and positions in international organizations. Our system of loyalty clearances and prior investigations often caused crippling delays before an American became eligible to accept a job on any of the numerous world bodies to which we belong. As a result, this aspect of our postwar security program completely defeated itself. It is much easier for an international organization to hire a foreign Communist or other enemy of our country than an American. Americans cannot be cleared for many weeks, or months. Therefore, we have continually lost opportunities to place our own citizens in responsible positions offered them.

An American heading an important international agency complained: "It would be far simpler for me to hire any Russian than an American when I have a vacancy to fill. There isn't the slightest security aspect to this particular organization. Yet it took Washington, working on a rush basis, six weeks to clear me for my job—despite the years I had previously spent in government service. I have on my staff a former United States federal security officer. It took eight weeks to clear him. It sometimes requires from six to nine months for American citizens to have their loyalty checked. As a result, international agencies—including my own—are led to search elsewhere for replacements. They need people in a hurry. I have had to rely heavily on Englishmen in positions I frequently would have preferred to make available to competent Americans. And many Americans who might be interested in international work simply don't want to face this humiliating security program and its inevitable delays. They get fed up and accept more profitable if less dedicated jobs."

This is not an isolated complaint. One of our principal security officials in Washington admitted to me: "We are losing ground in organizations like the United Nations where we could get people into good positions except for delays forced by clearance requirements. We have to let many positions go by the board where it would be advantageous to have an American employed. It is so much easier and speedier to find an available foreign national. This is particularly true of temporary commissions and short-run appointments. These are usually set up on a 'crash' basis. For example, if a UNESCO group wants experts for a three months' study of Haiti, it needs them immediately. It can't wait for our tedious clearance machinery to function."

A high State Department official protested that we are so careful to check the loyalty of our citizens destined for international jobs that vacancies are sometimes instead filled by foreign Communists who are at hand. He expressed the opinion that our complex security system is at last improving. Nevertheless, he said that it is still often self-defeating and highly embarrassing. "It is most mortifying," he added, "to have American security agents going around interrogating the families, friends, and acquaintances of respectable American citizens in foreign countries. This gives the implication that they have committed a crime."

The latest State Department list of international organizations to which the United States belongs gives a total of sixtynine. In 1954, we contributed almost $100,000,000 to their operation. Not quite 3,000 Americans work for twelve major agencies, such as the United Nations and the World Bank. They are cleared for such positions under a different security directive from that which applies to employees of the United States government. Only their loyalty is scrutinized. Government employees are also subjected to checks on unrelated "suitability factors."

The loyalty of applicants for international jobs is determined under two presidential executive orders by an International Organizations Employes Loyalty Board. This is an element of the Civil Service Commission. But the board cannot begin to act until a laborious check through F.B.I., Central Intelligence Agency, police, and other records has been completed. Undoubtedly the problems involved are immensely complex. It is logical that the United States should not desire to have traitors representing us on international agencies. But it is certainly sheer lunacy to devise a system for preventing this that is merely self-destroying. As things now stand, it is easier for a Russian to get a job on a U.N. commission than an American. Our efforts to keep out United States Communists open the doors to Soviet Communists. Surely this makes no sense. The same craving for security unfortunately developed in the State Department into one of the most famous witch hunts of the McCarthy era. This managed to damage severely our Foreign Service. Indeed, the unusually competent China Language Service was castrated. To satisfy the Know-Nothing wing of the Republican party, Dulles permitted a hatchet man, inflicted upon him by Senator Styles Bridges, to destroy one of the finest divisions of our diplomatic branch. The name of this hatchet man was Scott McLeod. He was rewarded for his activities by being named ambassador to Eire.

That period was typified by the brutally unfair treatment of John Paton Davies, Jr., a distinguished American diplomat. His persecution had a profound and gloomy effect upon the morale of the United States Foreign Service, which comprises those career diplomats whose intelligence, vision, and reliability in analyzing world affairs represent our first line of defense. A conviction began to prevail among many of these exceptionally important government servants abroad that they were being cynically sacrificed to the passions of political second-guessers. Sentiments fomented against them were often based upon the appetite of McCarthyism and a cheap desire to offer up to popular ignorance anybody who could be proved to have guessed wrong on world events in the past.

Despair developed among patriotic and sincere American diplomats. They could not understand how a man who professed to be so scrupulously moral and avowedly just as Dulles could lend himself to this miserable purge. Davies, hounded for several years, was well and favorably known among his colleagues. An exceptionally hard-working man, he took the trouble to learn the languages of China and Russia. Disillusioned by the corrupt cynicism of Chiang Kai-shek's government during World War II, he tended to sympathize with the Mao Tse-tung Communist movement.

If he misread the ultimate implications of Mao, he was far from alone in that error. By way of contrast, Moscow both underestimated and mistrusted Mao at the time Davies was in China. Davies's later reporting from Moscow and Bonn was not only brilliant but impeccable, even in the light of present "Monday-morning-quarterback" methods of analysis. That he advocated a course of "let the dust settle first" before Wash-

ington devised a new China policy is well known. This stratagem certainly could not have been worse than some idiocies
advocated since then.

The injustice of the Davies case reflects upon the whole
fabric of American diplomacy. A well-known career ambassador admitted confidentially that he no longer dared report the
brazen truth because of the hysteria. This was a sad admission
by an otherwise integrious man. But that such pressure should
have arisen to expose his moral cowardice is even sadder. Our
Foreign Service was for a long time eroded. Henry M. Wriston,
President of Brown University and chairman of the Secretary
of State's Public Committee on Personnel, wrote: "It requires
courage to report a situation as a man sees it and then to take
the consequences." Unfortunately for the American people,
all but our bravest diplomats were encouraged to seek refuge
behind the camouflage of vagueness.

Great injustice was done, and continued to be done, under
the inept application of President Eisenhower's famous security decree—Executive Order 10450. On September 7, 1954,
a civil servant named Jesse M. MacKnight returned to his
important State Department job from a holiday. He found on
his desk a notice curtly suspending him without pay. He was
accused of contacts with Communist sympathizers, while he
was in the Justice Department some years back. MacKnight
was also charged with trying to "obstruct, hamper or nullify"
plans of the United States government to embarrass the Soviet
bloc. Actually, MacKnight was the State Department representative on an interdepartmental psychological warfare committee (the Operations Coordinating Board). He presented
the official State Department viewpoint (approved by Secretary Dulles). In this capacity he managed to frustrate some
especially crackpot Pentagon ideas.

The thought of "trying" American diplomats for past opinions or wrong guesses is abhorrent. Joseph Clark Grew, former
United States Ambassador to Japan, told me that under such

a system both he and the entire American Embassy in Berlin during World War I should have been purged. They initially reported that Germany had not been the aggressor.

In 1954 I had an interesting talk with McLeod, the much-debated young man who, after a career in the F.B.I., became boss of State Department security. McLeod is engaging and forthright. He sincerely believed that "security" was a basic criterion of diplomacy. Discussing the department's current program, McLeod referred frankly to the days when he used to investigate applicants for jobs in the F.B.I. After checking all other qualifications of a candidate, he used to think, said he: "How would I like him to be behind a tree with me in a gun fight? You get pretty high standards if you think along such lines. And that's the way I like to think in these investigations."

John Paton Davies, Jr., was but one of an embarrassingly long list of United States diplomats who would not fit behind a tree with Scott McLeod.

The purpose of ambassadors is to inform their governments on the course of events and to assist in their interpretation. It is a Soviet habit to encourage its diplomats to report only what Moscow desires to hear. Unfortunately, our own political climate for a time threatened to engender similar moods in the American Foreign Service.

Any attempt by politicians to punish envoys for unpopular opinions or to intrude emotional currents into the making of policy is particularly dangerous now that we are forced to rely so heavily upon practical diplomatic methods. One is reminded by the latter-day history of Athens of the dangers inherent in such pressures. The great city-state developed a coalition to oppose aggressive expansion. But, as Sir Harold Nicolson recounts, while King Philip of Macedon divided the alliance and plucked off one member after another, "the Assembly at Athens were condemning unsuccessful Ambassadors to death, holding turbulent sessions to discuss the dispatch of new embassies with fresh instructions, grasping at promises which they knew to be false or at hopes which they knew to be fallacious, and destroying such confidence as their allies still placed in their sagacity and fortitude."

It is of crucial importance that the United States should have an efficient and astute diplomatic service. No matter how much an agile secretary of state like Dulles may travel, it is from our envoys that we derive the daily information on which we must postulate policy decisions. Washington is now represented in foreign capitals almost entirely by ambassadors (seventy-seven out of eighty chiefs of mission). Indeed, there has been a great inflation in rank among our representatives. Before World War II, most United States chiefs of mission were ministers. The embassy or legation post of third secretary was an honorable position. At a time during the height of the postwar inflationary phase, when we had four ambassadors in Paris and even, for a moment, three in tiny Beirut, there was only one third secretary in our London Embassy.

Not only has there been inflation in rank, but important positions have unfortunately been downgraded. I have in mind particularly the post of ambassador to NATO. NATO is by far the most significant of our alliances and a principal pillar of U.S. policy. During the early years of our membership, we were represented in its permanent council by men of outstanding quality. But this level was eventually reduced.

Unfortunately, this occurred just as the alliance began to enter into a period of doldrums, thus giving the impression of less American interest. Instead of galvanizing public attention to NATO by naming as our envoy another man of international repute, we moved in the other direction. Even Dulles later complained that our ambassador was insufficiently informed by Washington and of inadequate stature. But he did nothing to rectify the situation.

American diplomats are almost all members of the career

Foreign Service, except for chiefs of mission. The majority of the latter are also career men; but there is always a considerable fraction of political appointees, often in extremely expensive posts like Paris and London, which few government servants can afford. These assignments are given as a reward to generous contributors in political campaigns, sometimes possessing socially ambitious wives or a taste for travel.

The United States has a right to be proud of many of its diplomats. Ambassadors of both the career and noncareer variety have been outstanding: men like Charles E. Bohlen, George Kennan, David Bruce, and Douglas Dillon. These are at least the equal in ability of the best emissaries from any other nation. Unfortunately, our system of political spoils, which rewards deserving party supporters with embassies, occasionally produces tragic results. These can redound to the discredit of our country. A deadhead Alabaman who had been secretary to his senator represented us in two countries just as they were about to be invaded. A prosperous businessman tarnished our reputation in two other lands. Both were Democratic appointees. And the famous recent instance of a politically appointed envoy in strategically located Ceylon does not bear repetition.

It is difficult to describe the qualifications for a good diplomat. Yusuf Khass Hajib, an adviser to the great Mongol khans, wrote in the year 1069: "A successful ambassador must know how to read and write. He should be able to read and recite poetry. He must have a beautiful handwriting and be able to read all types of script. . . . He must be skilled in astronomy . . . medicine . . . accounting . . . surveying and geometry . . . and in the science of interpreting dreams. . . . He must be skilled in games like cards, chess, polo, *jereed,* archery, and hunting, for these are a means of winning friends. . . . He must be an orator and fluent in many languages, for ambassadors perform their duties by means of words."

It is no longer requisite, fortunately, for an envoy to have all these qualifications, and I doubt if even the versatile Mr. Bohlen is adept at jereed. But intelligence, knowledge, and discretion are sometimes forgotten when we choose non-professional representatives. This leaves us in precisely the position Callières discovered in early eighteenth-century France: "And indeed we find that instead of gradual promotion by degrees and by the evidence of proved capacity and experience, as is the case in the usages of war, one may see often men who have never left their own country, who have never applied themselves to the study of public affairs, being of meager intelligence, appointed so to speak overnight to important embassies in countries of which they know neither the interests, the laws, the customs, the language, nor even the geographical situation."

It seems lunatic that the United States should not *always* exercise the same scrupulous care in choosing diplomats as it does, shall we say, in selecting generals. But our democracy still displays insufficient interest in foreign relationships. Foreigners, after all, do not vote. George Kennan has observed that there is an evident "unsuitability of the American Governmental system for the promulgation of any sustained administrative program (particularly one calling for annual appropriation of sizeable sums of money) that was not supported at all times by the enthusiasm of some interested domestic pressure group."

Our career diplomats themselves are insufficiently trained as far as linguistic competence is concerned and often inadequately paid to meet the obvious social obligations of representing a great nation in distant lands. For example, a survey in 1956 showed that we had only one Foreign Service officer who spoke Turkish, only three rated fluent in Arabic, and only three similarly rated in Chinese. This is not good enough. Our professionals are drawn from a highly literate population of 170,000,000 people. It is particularly distressing if we stop to consider that the diplomatic service of our great opponent, Russia, abounds in talented linguists. Asia's capitals are filled with Soviet emissaries who speak the native tongue fluently as well as English, the lingua franca of the East.

And our representatives are often not able to fly the flag properly because of niggardly treatment by Congress. We spend less than .00135 per cent of the total annual budget to pay representation expenses for these diplomats. It is all the State Department can do to convince the legislators that even this pittance is necessary. There is a curious tradition in American folklore that those who labor for us overseas are dilettantes who merit minimal financial reward. This is shockingly untrue. Nevertheless, since diplomatists are less complicated machines than guided missiles, requests to succor them provoke Congressional sarcasms about the sybaritic tastes of gentlemen in striped pants.

There are, as described above, two species of envoy: career and political. The former is selected on the basis of survival capacities of brain and liver. The latter is chosen on the basis of bank account—and how much of it is made available to the administration currently in office. Robert McClintock, our Chief of Mission in Beirut and a veteran Foreign Service officer, has made an earnest investigation of both categories. He observes: " 'What makes ambassadors?' is the question heard almost as frequently as 'Who makes ambassadors?' 'Why are ambassadors made?' is a question to which each chargé d'affaires ad interim thinks he has the answer. It will suffice for the purpose of this general study to say that by and large professional ambassadors get that way after a much longer period of gestation (accompanied at times by violent prenatal movements and kicks) than political ambassadors, who occasionally step full-fledged from the forehead of the President. During this period the former are usually handled with less care than the latter but need less care later."

Certainly one respect in which careerists need more care is that of expense accounts. A well-heeled individual whose ambitious wife has induced him to finance his party's National Committee and thereby qualify as diplomat is likely to feel generous enough to accept with pleasure that occupation's entertainment obligations. Such, unfortunately, is not always the case with the professional, who has no money of his own. Congress is stingy in making up the deficit.

The United States is the world's wealthiest country. Its citizens are proud of their reputation for generous hospitality. Business executives and even lesser employees are encouraged to charge on expense accounts all manner of representation in the name of better contacts. And the United States Treasury permits this.

The State Department would like to be equally generous. After all, as the frequently cited Callières wrote: "It is in the nature of things that good cheer is a great conciliator, that it fosters familiarity and promotes freedom of exchange between the guests, while the warmth of wine will often lead to the discovery of important secrets."

But not, alas, in many of the embassies, legations, and consulates of Uncle Sam. The last Congress approved only a minimal amount for diplomatic entertaining this fiscal year. Surely, considering the amount of whisky consumed by junketing Congressmen in the homes of our diplomatists, the request for more expense money is not unreasonable. Our professional, as distinct from political, envoys are no longer a prosperous group. This is a result of the democratization of our Foreign Service. Rich politicos are necessary because, for example, the American ambassador in Paris pays half his household maintenance and two-thirds of his hospitality costs from his own pocket.

From all over the globe, American career diplomats complain they are going broke while colleagues from poorer lands outdo them in splendid entertainment. Allowances, carefully rationed by the State Department after the Congressional hatchet has descended, usually vanish after a few months. Then our agents must choose between personal destitution or temporary disappearance from the social scene. It is thus not infrequent that some envoys devise penny-pinching means regarded as odd by colleagues.

McClintock studied one of these methods. He said: "Cases of precocious aridity, or ambassadorial siccation, have been described which showed what painful effects can be associated with this phenomenon. Usually the eyeballs of guests at table become covered with a glaucous glaze, and an anhydrous effect is present; conversation wanes and an acute attack of spoonfoggles is diagnosed. ('Spoonfoggles' is an early Mississippi word characterizing intense desire for drink.) On one occasion in one of the larger embassies where the Ambassador served only ice water, an Italian diplomat whispered while the Ambassador was saying grace: 'I hope he is praying for the miracle of turning water into wine.' "

A more practical prayer could have been addressed to the United States legislature. It is time Congress awakened to our need for social self-respect. The State Department is frequently kicked by Capitol Hill. But there is no sense starving it—or at least its foreign guests.

No matter which party is in power, who is president, and who is secretary of state, the United States depends heavily upon the intelligence, vision, and reliability of its envoys. Its attitudes on foreign affairs are influenced to a considerable degree by the judgment of these diplomats as collated and evalued by the State Department and National Security Council.

It is, therefore, of utmost importance that we exercise care in the appointment of suitable ambassadors. Policy is fundamentally based upon the act of weighing probabilities. This is especially true of United States policy, which continues to be largely empirical. Why, then, are we so careless about selecting those who represent us? Why are we, the wealthiest country, so niggardly about paying adequate allowances to envoys—with the result that often we send inexperienced rich amateurs to most important capitals? And even with competent amateurs, Washington is not always wise in distributing them most suitably. Thus, for example, Bruce, one of our French-speaking statesmen, is now in Bonn. He knows no German. The envoy in Paris, Amory Houghton, understands German but has only a smattering of French. The Chief of Mission in Rome does not speak Italian. Linguistic talent is not everything, but surely it is possible to find wealthy men who comprehend the better-known foreign tongues.

In the professional Foreign Service we are fortunate in having some outstanding individuals. But we do not make the best use of available ability. Thus Bohlen, an outstanding Soviet expert, was shunted to Manila. He could serve far better in a position concerned with Communist affairs. The Dulles regime has railroaded out some of our finest talent— men like Kennan, Davies, and Charles Thayer. This in itself is ridiculous. But it is positively shocking that the police agent chosen for such dirty work, McLeod, should have been rewarded by being named ambassador to Ireland. The choice is an insult to the Irish and to American common sense.

Is it not time sanity and order were applied to our Foreign Service? Certainly enough money should be made available to the State Department to enable any man to accept any assignment. Certainly, also, we should try to select envoys who know the simpler and more widely spoken languages. Certainly we should employ specialists where they are best suited. And certainly we should cease exporting hacks or hatchet men as a reward for electoral bets or dirty work.

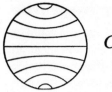 *Chapter 3*

Seeing Ourselves as Others See Us

The United States has lost the initiative in its propaganda contest with the Soviet bloc. Recently we have gone from defeat to defeat. It is not merely a question of winning the allegiance, or at least the tolerance, of uncommitted peoples. We are no longer even successfully galvanizing the attention of allied populations. This situation, already unfortunate, could become tragic if it is not corrected. It stems more from carelessness and stupidity on our part than from any special Russian brilliance or technique.

Propaganda, a word that embarrasses us, is one of the most important cold-war weapons. We have paid inadequate attention to this fact. Continually, we allow Moscow to appear to take the lead in what is made to seem a quest for peace. Public opinion everywhere is desperately eager that this quest be pursued. But we, by inept explanation of our views, permit ourselves to seem lagging and reluctant. Dulles emerged as a kind of tragicomic figure, the greatest No Man since Molotov was in his prime. He let himself seem to accept diplomatic paralysis as an act of faith.

We have tended for years to be vague and even inaccurate in advertising our viewpoints. And we have helplessly watched the Russians, like cuckoo birds, invade our ideological nest and make off with some of its most precious eggs. We continually bill the struggle for power as one between West and East or between Democracy and Communism. But in reality it is a contest between independent and serf nations, between those favoring, not "coexistence" (a murky word invented by Lenin and Stalin), but peace and those seeking violent change. When we loosely refer to "East-West" differences we almost deliberately let Moscow appear by inference as champion of the Oriental world, much of which we would protect.

And we are foolish to insist on ideological terms. Neither Turkey nor Portugal, two of the NATO allies, even faintly resembles Jeffersonian democracy. Yet they are entitled to full protection. Yugoslavia is Communist; nevertheless it is not our enemy in the sense that Russia is. It should not be too difficult to use more exact semantics. But it is harder to recapture our own most valuable words, so shrewdly pirated by Moscow: "democracy," "freedom," and "justice."

The Soviets grabbed these, extracted their real meaning, and stuffed them with falsehood. Then they reproclaimed them to the world as Communist beliefs. General Marshall, as Secretary of State, challenged Molotov to define "democracy." He was never answered. The cuckoo has not entirely spirited the eggs away; but he has spoiled and soiled them. Yet, enough words remain in the lexicon for us to explain our principles and aims. This is not being done successfully. We talk too much about the prosperity of our system. Men do not fight for living standards but for a way of life. Too often our propaganda is conceived in terms both comprehensible and pleasing to ourselves. However, its purpose is largely to imprint ideas on distant peoples with foreign minds and different traditions. We must inspire others rather than proclaim how satisfied we are with our own comfortable civilization. This is a time of change. And if we would have the change go our way, we must capture men's imagination—particularly the imagination of youth, for youth in a time of change is all-important.

Soviet propaganda seeks to convey the impression of a basic logic that progresses unalterably toward an inescapable end. Lenin, who brilliantly grasped what was helpful to him in Marx, taught that "propaganda is of crucial importance." Modern means of applying this dictum have been carefully co-ordinated by the Moscow monolith. But it is questionable whether our propaganda has successfully faced this challenge. The West German government has published a commentary complaining that we emphasize material things too much. We have allowed the initiative in the realm of spiritual ideas to remain largely in the very materialistic hands of Communism.

"Are we," asks Bonn, "ready for this spiritual competition? Do we understand the system of thought, belief and ideology of the East? Do we have any certitude about the basis of our lives and our faith? Ideological faith in the collectivist idea makes the Soviet man capable of achievements and sacrifices that surpass human strength. Only a faith that in no way is dependent on material events, that does not live in expectation of future well-being, can resist this ideology. This faith, this conviction must inspire Western man to risk his life for the ultimate values that cannot be abandoned—freedom, personal dignity, the lives of other men, the truth of religion."

There is no sign that the powers of the West have sought seriously to analyze the problem of their propaganda and to co-ordinate efforts in presenting their case abroad. We remain constantly on the defensive, permitting the Kremlin's experts to exploit the very evident chinks in our imperfect armor. Only when Moscow acts openly with brutal menace do the free powers respond in concert and remember that the essential contradictions of our time are those between themselves and Communism. In periods of relaxation we tend to forget the need to reassert constantly the inner meaning of our ideology. This is a dangerous lack. Surely there are enough beneficial aspects in the democratic system, whatever imperfections it may have, to merit retelling to the point of redundancy.

Simple facts bear frequent repetition. As I said earlier, Pericles told Athens: "We are superior to our enemies . . . our city is open to the world . . . we live freely, and yet we face the same dangers as readily as they . . . those men surely should be deemed bravest who know most clearly what danger is and what pleasure is and are not made thereby to flinch."

The Soviet sputniks undoubtedly stimulated a spasm of new thinking in the West. Because of this, we may regard Russia's scientific triumph as beneficial to ourselves. Ideas are beginning to sprout in what was for too long a fallow field. But the democratic populations crave inspiration from their governments. Such inspiration is slow in coming. For all too long, Western statesmen have been complacent about the support their peoples are prepared to give them. A danger exists that their lead will not be followed unless it becomes more positive and magnetic.

Although our principal alliance, NATO, was started as a military confederation, that was not its sole purpose. It sought to be a completely novel experiment in co-operation, which could expose Russia as an isolated, reactionary state. This image has become confused. There have been great changes to which NATO has not adjusted. The alliance, whose purpose was to build up enough strength to negotiate, has never given sufficient attention to how, when, or on what to bargain.

For too long, we failed to pursue our own imaginative initiative. We have been forced, therefore, to answer Soviet diplomatic moves and propaganda with rebuttals rather than fresh declarations of our own. We cannot afford to reply to every lie propounded by the highly productive Moscow publicity system. We would simply have no time left for developing our own story. George Kennan suggests: "A wise Western policy will insist that no single falsehood or distortion from the Soviet side should ever go unanswered. This will be tiresome. We do not like repetition. But we cannot afford to dispense with it. Truth does not win over error just on its merits. It, too, has to be assiduously propagated."

Kennan is right in his conclusion but wrong in the methods he recommends. We simply cannot retort to every Moscow misstatement. There is not enough radio time. Our propaganda would find itself at the same disadvantage suffered for so long by our diplomacy: confining itself to negative responses. We must emphasize with clarity the positive aspects of our story. We must convince our own populations that this is a time to spend more on guns than on butter.

We must reassure everyone that we are making every reasonable effort to relax tension, but if the Russians are not themselves reasonable we are determined to defend our interests. Nevertheless, we cannot give the impression, as sometimes is unfortunately done, that we are not ready to talk about peace.

In depicting ourselves abroad we often ignore the real appeal of our way of life, which remains young, vigorous, and attractive to others in a political and spiritual sense. We err when we stress material things and get into the wrong kind of contest with another kind of materialism. We do not take enough pains in presenting our aid programs to underdeveloped lands. There is little point in offering help just "to defeat Communism." This patently means assistance is really designed to strengthen ourselves. We must honestly recognize that poverty unchallenged is a disgrace.

Likewise, we tell Europe we wish to accelerate defense measures because of the increased menace of extinction brought about by techniques symbolized by sputnik. Europe is not particularly impressed. The Continent has been living under the menace of extinction for a decade. What sputnik and ICBMs mean is that the threat has suddenly been brought home to the United States.

We must begin in this post-sputnik survival race to re-examine propaganda approaches and suit them better to those of our adversary. Let us indeed stick to the truth. Neither France's Henri IV nor our own Benjamin Franklin was wrong in conceiving honesty as the best policy. But let us also make more attractive what we have to tell. Let us cease thinking of this primarily in terms that please ourselves. We must comprehend the wants of other, distant audiences. Where Moscow has gained a great lead is by applying to its political warfare the principle of market analysis. Each country's tastes and hopes are studied. Surely market analysis is something at which our trading nation should be expert.

Propaganda is a recognized and increasingly important branch of foreign policy. By its adept use we should endeavor to impress the validity of our views and the value of our principles upon the peoples of other nations with whom we would live in peace. In this respect, it is imperative that we co-ordinate the tale we tell with the actions we take or intend to take. Thus, we must never mislead captive peoples, as in Hungary, to the extent that they may rely upon our help if they revolt—when we do not contemplate giving such aid. Nor, on the other hand, can we afford totally to ignore subjected friends who still cherish thoughts of future liberty.

In some respects, the only safe course is to remind enslaved peoples that freedom is a viable commodity in large portions of the world and to portray how it functions in our own land. But it is impossible to give an accurate picture to foreign audiences of the extraordinary pattern of civilization we have developed here during the seventeen decades since our own revolution. Our political ideas are, for the most part, somewhat abstract, and they date directly back to the main streams of philosophy through Jefferson, Voltaire, and Montesquieu all the way to the Athenians. These conceptions, so thoroughly understood by peoples to whom the habits of democracy are indigenous, are difficult to crystallize and transmit abroad for propaganda purposes. Furthermore, that comfortable amalgam we call "the American way of life" is almost incomprehensible to many foreign populations accustomed for generations to struggle for mere existence and a modicum of liberty.

How can one describe to the outer world the vivid contrasts of this country? Pennsylvania farmers in red hunting caps ambling outside busy industrial towns while their bird dogs cast the fields for quail and pheasant. West Virginia miners riding away from coal tipples in brand-new automobiles. Earnest clubwomen in Louisville fingering pretentious hats and arguing whether the Republican party is the only living expression of Jefferson's ideas. The russet deciduous forests of north Tennessee and the tang of fresh sawdust heaped up by the mills. And, in the wide Baptist belt, the constant broadcasting of hillbilly hymns with their cozy medieval intimacy with the divine hierarchy.

Although in the South racism's horror still persists acutely and even in the Border States political allegiance is all too often rooted in whether one's ancestors "shot for the North" or not, there is, despite sharp regional differences, a strange unity of custom and opinion vis-à-vis the outer world. This kind of impression is hard to convey abroad. But it plays a part in that strange modern medium known as political warfare.

An expert in the latter medium, Professor Hugh Seton-Watson, a distinguished English student of East European languages and history, once prepared an analysis of the operations of Radio Free Europe, a privately financed organization which with the Voice of America comprises our best-known propaganda operation behind the Iron Curtain. Asked as an impartial expert to make this report, he observes: "It is a clear lesson of the history of the last thirty years that totalitarian regimes create internal and external conflicts that are bound to damage peace. The nature of the present (satellite) regimes excludes any means of communication other than those used by Free Europe—namely, broadcasts (and) balloon-borne leaflets."

'Despite complaints about these activities from Moscow and its puppets, Seton-Watson recommended they should not be suspended unless: the U.S.S.R. ceases to behave as the West's enemy; one or more of the satellites separate themselves from Soviet control at least as effectively as Yugoslavia; or a national Communist government permits its citizens much greater freedom of thought, speech, travel, and contact with the West. In certain countries these conditions may eventually be met. Nevertheless, Seton-Watson reasons: "Pressure and the threat of pressure from below are needed to push them further along the path toward independence. Any strengthening of that mood is helpful. In so far as leaflets contribute to strengthening it, they help rather than hinder political evolution." This is a sound description of one propaganda function.

Nevertheless, it is not just by official and unofficial (if government-assisted) radio programs abroad that we provide others with their picture of America. Travelers, books, plays, and, above all, the cinema contribute an important share. In fact, millions of people in this world know nothing of the United States but what they see in the movies. Hollywood is the looking glass in which is reflected the American way of life, its philosophy and ideology. Willy-nilly, the film industry has come to be a signally important if unintended arm of policy, for its unconscious propaganda effect upon foreign minds is immense.

This is now acknowledged by agencies dealing with our affairs overseas. In times of emergency, efforts have been made to influence the manufacture and distribution of movies in accordance with policy shifts. During World War II the export of "Mr. Smith Goes to Washington" was held up for fear it might prejudice the nation's war effort. When we were military allies of the U.S.S.R., the State Department urged production of pro-Soviet films such as "North Star" and "Mission to Moscow." When "Grapes of Wrath," dealing with the tragic situation of itinerant farmers, was first released, the United States Embassy in France requested that it be withheld from that country on the grounds that it might assist Communist propaganda efforts. Instead, the producer inserted a special preface explaining that the situation described had now been corrected. During the critical 1948 elections in Italy, the movie "Ninotchka" was widely distributed at the State Department's request to encourage anti-Communist voters by ridicule of the Soviet system.

But the government has no tangible control over the film industry. When the United States Information Agency wants to produce an outright propaganda movie such as "Poles Are Stubborn People" it merely asks Hollywood to manufacture a movie from an official script. Occasionally Washington will informally suggest subjects. When she was an ambassador, Clare Boothe Luce proposed a film on the diplomatic service. But the producer who was approached concluded that available plot material was not very exciting. General Curtis E. Lemay inspired the movie on our long-range bombers, "Strategic Air Command," and the State Department saw to it that this was displayed at a Berlin festival.

Unfortunately, the reflection of ourselves presented by Hollywood is sometimes not entirely what we would like. Above all, an impression of thoughtlessness and brutality is often conveyed to the foreign mind. During the past few years, national censorships have deleted from American movies scenes considered too brutal in England, Norway, Sweden, Belgium, the Netherlands, West Germany, Australia, New Zealand, India, and Indonesia. In 1953 word was spread among major studios suggesting that scenes of physical violence be toned down in order to avoid giving the world too savage a portrait of the United States.

Hollywood is concerned with its unsought role as unofficial

propaganda center. The chairman of the Motion Picture Association observes: "Poor patriotism is bad business." The industry depends for its economic survival upon foreign markets. For every dollar it earns in the United States, another forty-five cents comes from abroad. Were this figure to be cut substantially, the industry might collapse. As a result, the makers of movies are particularly concerned about not hurting foreign feelings. Mexicans, who used to be cast as villains or idlers, are now assigned more dashing roles. A recent film calling for two Brazilian wastrels was re-edited to avoid offending South Americans.

It is far easier to refrain from injuring the sensibilities of other nations than it is to present ourselves in a particularly sympathetic way. The very films that audiences most enjoy as escapist entertainment—such as crime or Wild West pictures—are those that contribute to our violent reputation. The British censor who cut scenes out of the recent "From Here to Eternity" remarked: "This shows your army in much too unfavorable a light for our audiences. Our alliance with you is too important to permit this."

In fact, depicting ourselves for the outer world is in part a tricky process because the outer world does not necessarily *like* us; not even some of our truest political friends do. Particularly because we are a mercantile power whose businessmen insist that their government protect their interests, we suffer the criticisms once directed at mercantile Athens. Its great cynic, Demosthenes, said: "Our purposes and our actions must invariably be just. Yet we must be careful to see that they are also attended with advantage." The measure of that "advantage" demanded by our Congress in Washington often seems exorbitantly high in Oslo, London, or Tokyo.

The resulting clash of business interests cannot but dim the bright portrait of ourselves and our good intentions that we endeavor to present. Throughout the allied world one finds repercussions of this fact. For example, like members of an energetic family, Britain and America are given to periods of mutual irritation. That we fought side by side in two destructive wars and shared responsibility in many another crisis never wholly obscured latent differences in outlook on the two sides of the Atlantic. These differences are plainly discerned because of common heritage and language.

Today there is little doubt that vague anti-Americanism is evident in England. In no sense is it a major factor, nor does it obtrude in personal relationships. Exceedingly forthright discussions can be—and are—held with never a letdown in the impeccable courtesy traditional to that island. But the veil of good manners cannot obscure the development of a somewhat acerb mood toward ourselves. Randolph Churchill, a prominent British journalist, believes: "In this country there are two forms of anti-Americanism and in both cases the main bulk of the resentment felt is, like the bulk of an iceberg, submerged. Many Socialists cannot forgive the Americans for making such a triumphant success of the capitalist system. Many Tories find it hard to forgive America for becoming 'top nation.' Even quite intelligent people in both parties, who recognize that these prejudices are ill-founded and absurd and who are sensible enough not to utter them in public, are none-the-less the secret victims of them."

The Labor bias to which Churchill refers is associated primarily with the leftist wing of Aneurin Bevan, although by no means solely confined to that. The Conservative attitude is less easily isolated and is founded largely upon emotion. One might say it dates back to Woodrow Wilson and his theories of national self-determination, which, in a philosophical sense, have contributed far more than we realize to the gradual disintegration of the British Empire.

Many Tories have not yet adjusted themselves to the great trend of nationalism and what both we and the Russians are inclined to call anticolonialism—respectively forgetting our own land-girt or overseas territorial possessions. Some of these

same Tories, seeing the national wealth diminish with Britain's
Empire, resent, too, what they term "dollar imperialism."
These vague currents were shaping up for years while Americans vociferously pressed for Irish and Indian independence.
They came to a sharp head over the Middle East and Cyprus.
An astonishing number of Englishmen hold Washington responsible for weakening Britain in Iran, forcing abandon-
ment of the Suez Canal base, urging the Sudan toward
independence, and the failure of Americans to comprehend
Britain's attitude on Cyprus. This mood induces various suspicions. Some politicians fear London will someday be ignored
by Washington in an eventual direct deal with Moscow. Others
feel we are brashly disregarding British experience and com-
placently leading the world toward trouble.

In France it is not difficult to encounter similar resentment.
Before World War II, I once engaged in argument with the
buxom, faintly mustachioed *patronne* of a small Paris *bistro*.
"Ah," said she by way of summing up, "you Americans were
chics in 1917—not now." We who were chic in 1917 and
again a quarter of a century later are no longer so popular
among the French. On both extreme Left and extreme Right
an ugly current of anti-American feeling is running. Why?

In contemplating the problem we would do well to restrain
any self-righteous tendency to boast of the help we gave
France during and after two conflicts. People do not become
"anti" anything without some reason. What is the reason that
has prompted growing distaste for us in a country that is our
oldest ally and dearest Continental friend? One obvious factor
is the change in status of the United States and France.
Forty years ago we ranked approximately sixth among
the world's powers, while France boasted the "finest army in
Europe" and an immense empire. During World War I we
played a relatively minor part. Our troops came under the over-
all command of Marshal Ferdinand Foch and were largely
equipped with French guns, aircraft, and transport.

No nation likes to see itself slipping on the scale of grandeur. It is human nature to resent those that replace it. The mere fact that we regard ourselves as France's benefactors, who contributed blood and treasure to restoring her equilibrium, is no compensation for damaged pride. Few people adore their benefactors. This background existed long before Paris politicians began to assert that in Indochina and North Africa we worked to oust French authority in order to establish our own hegemony—an asseveration that does not lose force because it is untrue. It preceded complaints that we opposed France at Suez and sent small arms to Tunisia. Already in 1954 General de Gaulle predicted to me that the mounting crisis would inevitably result in xenophobia, directed, above all, at Americans. The following year he was saying: "There is no hate for the United States in France. France remains friendly to the United States. But the French people don't like the American people."

André Fontaine, a distinguished Paris journalist, recently analyzed anti-Americanism. He observed that relatively few Europeans know the United States by personal experience. Most depend upon an impression exported in the form of films, books, soldiers, businessmen, and tourists. Too frequently these bring to mind the wartime British complaint: "The trouble with you Yanks is that you're overpaid, oversexed, and over here."

Fontaine said our garrisons and travelers "cut themselves off. Hygiene and air conditioning separate them from the rest of the world. They drink Coca-Cola among the most magnificent vineyards." He believed Americans too often live in ostentatious luxury among their poorer allies, and our troops' "arrogance and lavish spending" provoke resentment and envy. This is confirmed in a similar study by Professor Leo Moulin of Brussels University. He says such conceptions are deliberately exaggerated by European intellectuals, who delight in false comparisons between the "Florentine artisan" and the "dehumanization of the American robot bound to the production line." Many of the so-called Continental intelligentsia prefer to identify the American way of life, says Professor Moulin, with "certain of its most extravagant and painful manifestations: rock and roll, the juke box, the strip-tease, stock car races, Westerns and thrillers, the delirium of jazz and baseball fans, the adoration of idols (James Dean or Marilyn Monroe), petting and the juvenile delinquent."

But it is not only high-brows, looking down supercilious noses, nor only the obviously anti-American Communists and fellow travelers, nor only those Right-Wingers who have never even accepted republicanism in France, who fan the present mood. It is a combination of all. The Left dislikes us as the epitome of capitalism. The Right dislikes us almost for the reverse: a distorted image of liberal, New Deal democracy. The intellectuals choose to consider us uncouth. The poor are indignant at our wealth. And the rich choose to believe that we intend to oust them from such properties as the Algerian oil fields.

Beyond this is the very human tendency to blame others for one's own unhappy lot. Such anti-Americanism as exists in France—and it is not yet a major force—is the kind of prejudice that throughout history has always been attached to big powers. Britain learned this, and Britain learned to ignore it. We must be prepared to do likewise. It may come as a shock to Americans who have made personal sacrifices to help our traditional allies, England and France, that we are by no means universally liked for such help. Fortunately, the tendency to carp at Americans seems to have declined somewhat in recent months as a consequence of the British economic recovery and the French political rebirth. And it is by now probably less of a surprise to know that in large segments of the politically uncommitted world we are looked upon with envy, resentment, and disdain.

The United States is not popular in India for reasons both

political and psychological. Neither country has a particularly acute understanding of the other. The result is, as one distinguished Indian says, "a touch of a sneer on both sides." A factor that contributes heavily is the attitude of Nehru. As a child he was influenced by an English governess who did not like Americans and taught that they were vulgar, second-rate people. He regards us generally as too materialist and insufficiently intellectual. Many of our ways irritate him. When he visited New York and Washington in 1949, he felt there was too much ostentation. He shuddered when a banker boasted about how many billions of dollars were represented at a luncheon in Nehru's honor. He was irked at an official banquet when two national leaders ignored him in favor of a discussion on the merits of bourbon whisky.

In political terms, the Republican administration is less liked by New Delhi than its Democratic predecessors were. Acheson made no secret of his belief that India was of vast importance. He regarded Nehru as the key man without whom the country would collapse. He felt there was no need to force him to be on our side; that he was doing enough merely by surviving. But the Republicans have shown irritation with Nehru. Irritation reacts in New Delhi with the effect of strong curry on an ulcer. Dulles is held responsible for our policy of giving military assistance to Pakistan.

Indians resent the attitude of many Americans toward colored peoples. They do not realize the progress made in eliminating this blemish—similar to India's efforts to scrap its discriminatory system of castes and outcastes. Because we are allied with the British and the French, we are regarded as sympathetic to colonialism. And because we are now the dominant Western power, we are seen as the real imperialists.

Hindu extremists cannot see why we want to bolster up Moslem Pakistan and Middle Eastern states. "They would collapse at the first sign of trouble," it is argued. "Why does the world's most powerful democracy have to depend on the corrupt and medieval countries?" C. D. Deshmukh, former Minister of Finance and one of the ablest men in India, puts the problem this way: "We don't misunderstand your motives, but you *are* helping colonialism—just as you say we are helping Communism by our actions. There are honest differences of opinion in our attitudes. You feel we are walking into the spider's parlor. We feel you are wrong in the assumption that military power is needed to negotiate with Communism. We remember that you considered atomic intervention at Dienbienphu even though that was canceled. We fear that another time it may occur and that the same thing may happen to us, as the result of a distant explosion, as happened to the Japanese fishermen near Eniwetok. After all, too many people live in this part of the world."

Anything that helps Pakistan is disagreeable to India; the wounds of partition still smart. And Dulles is blamed for policies in Korea and Formosa that were already charted under the Democrats. Logic is not a strong point of the Indians, who revel in contradictions. One encounters anti-Americans among them who educate their children in the United States. The same man excoriates "racism" in America and then concedes that the democratic attitude of GIs in India during the war destroyed the last shreds of British racial snobbery.

There are mutual differences in national personality to be understood and misconceptions of policy to be explained. Some Indians resent our forthright manner. Others claim we are too bossy and attach too many conditions to our aid. Still others find our sense of humor heavy for their subtler tastes. The psychology of their country is as strange to us as is its flair for brilliant colors or the fragrant air imbued with spice, incense, and the tang of betel nut. The natural touchiness of the Indian, exhilarated by a growing global role, is offended by anything even hinting at an attitude of racial superiority.

Any crackpot speech on white supremacy in our own country sends a damaging shudder across India.

This deep-seated racial complex is at the heart of any Asian or African opinion of things American. The press in newly independent states like India and Ghana reports with an almost wicked fascination on the agonies of our efforts to achieve for our own Negroes the democracy we would offer to the world. Even in ancient lands like Japan there are unpleasant, if well-concealed, resentments whenever our own darker citizens are mistreated. Official Japan's attitude toward these conflicts in the United States is best symbolized by the famous original three monkeys carved upon a frieze adorning the venerable Toshogu Shrine at Nikko. This trio, while gazing benignly from a holy mountain, refuses to either hear, speak, or see evil.

The inscrutable politeness of such sacred symbols has been observed by the Japanese in their formal contacts with American visitors ever since the horrors of bigotry were revived in their most sordid form in Arkansas. Through instinct and through custom Japan is a most courteous nation. Therefore, its representatives have gone out of their way to avoid adding to our obvious embarrassment. But in no sense should discretion be interpreted as a sign of disinterest. Japan, like other Asian lands, is acutely and emotionally concerned. It is not too much to say that our relationships with that country or, for that matter, with any Oriental peoples will never rest upon a comfortable psychological foundation until we have more clearly erased the racist stain from our national conscience.

Japan itself, like India, has not been entirely free of similar blots. During its long militaristic era, a fierce form of assumed superiority was permitted to develop. Even today, as some Tokyo newspapers have generously pointed out, three million "untouchables" of the Eta caste suffer from inequality and prejudice. But such self-conscious reminders of local weaknesses have in no sense obscured our own. The most sympathetic editorials take pains to remind us: "With things as they are, the United States cannot talk too loudly about humanitarianism." American prestige has been perceptibly diminished by what is labeled our "incurable disease."

Since the Supreme Court's original decision on integration, there had been a quiet rise in our reputation on this sensitive issue, so frustrating and so vital to true intercontinental understanding. But despite President Eisenhower's strong attitude, which has been observed with sympathy if incomplete comprehension of our political structure, the cancer of Little Rock has eaten deeply into the moral fiber of our cause.

The resolute justice of Eisenhower's personal position has done something to affirm in the East that we intend to rule ourselves by egalitarian law. Thus, there is a positive aspect to the problem. Even so critical a man as Krishna Menon was fair enough to admit as much. Still, this is far outweighed and overshadowed by the tarnish that has spread across the luster of our reputation from Seoul to Singapore and Suez.

The simple truth of the matter is that any moral gains we may have registered by our painfully just position during the 1956 Egyptian crisis and as a consequence of Soviet brutality in Hungary have now been largely obliterated. Budapest is far, far away from the people of Asia. Most of them are equally unfamiliar with the ideologies of Marx and Jefferson. But all of them have skins colored differently from that of Governor Orval Faubus. Our friends in the Orient are not going to cease doing business with us or relying upon us for support. Nevertheless, for a long time to come it will be difficult for us to preach with full acceptance that creed of equality and freedom among men which the government in Washington, if not the rabble of Little Rock, has sought so painstakingly to practice.

The issue that links the so-called Afro-Asian powers is to a large degree the pernicious one of color. The notion of white supremacy is not dead among Westerners in Africa and Asia. Hatred and suspicion of such a prejudice are vigorously alive on both continents. Communism has taken advantage of this situation. Its propaganda seeks to describe a United States that has assumed the mantle of colonialism and encourages racial discrimination. This kind of propaganda has considerable success. The revolutions now taking place in both Asia and Africa are psychological as well as political. New nations seek recognition of their pride and self-respect. And their intellectuals talk openly of ugly incidents that have occurred in the United States to people who do not have a fair skin.

Some years ago, the State Department began bringing selected foreigners to America on free tours. The idea was to demonstrate our way of life and build friendships among coming generations in distant lands. Unfortunately, many visitors have suffered embarrassment when faced abruptly with our race problem. Some, their pride hurt, have returned home distressed and convinced that we are at least "semicolonial" despite our protestations. This adds substance to Communist contentions. We have not done a forthright job in meeting the issue squarely. We have not explained adequately just what we have achieved in overcoming archaic prejudices or that the executive branch of our government actually takes the lead in trying to erase the blot of discrimination.

Willard Savoy, an American Negro, wrote some time ago in the *Reporter:* "Many of our friends in Asia are confused by our failure to meet communism's race-color Hate-America campaign face to face. They are unable to defend us against Communist charges and their confusion prevents Asians from thinking of us in terms of the freedom and better way of life that are Asia's objectives. Asia's revolution demands that the physical needs of its people be met *and* that their hunger for human dignity be satisfied. If we are to win the enduring allegiance of Asia's nations, we must help them find answers to both of these demands. We must tackle their doubts about us with the same realism that we are tackling their diseases."

One way of removing doubts is to accelerate our self-improvement on this embarrassing issue. That is a paramount necessity; it is intolerable that anyone could mention our democracy in the same sentence as South Africa's. Another is by giving encouragement to Negro leaders abroad.

Recently I discussed this with James F. Byrnes, a spokesman for Southern racial attitudes but also a former secretary of state aware of America's international responsibilities. He argued that the true facts of the Negro's position in the United States were not being reported fully either in the Northern press or abroad. Was the world aware, he inquired, that the Negro population of South Carolina alone, a poor state, possessed more automobiles than all the people of the U.S.S.R.?

"The Negroes have money," he continued. "They are in the banks, the stores, business. They are lawyers. They are making wonderful economic progress. But the people of the South cannot, on the other hand, be expected to change their way of life suddenly and accept Northern social concepts. There are deep, atavistic racial feelings in the South that cannot be suddenly swept away. But there is no such religious prejudice as exists among the three Arab nations who decline to let Jews enter their country. In our North there are hotels and clubs where no Jews are allowed. The people of New England who criticize us on the complex subject of racial integration fail to appreciate their own blind spots. We have a deep-seated racial problem which we do not wholly understand. This is terrible and sickening. Yet you cannot just solve it by decree. Look at the failure of Prohibition, which concerned mere appetites."

These remarks are worth pondering. They make plain how much more constant pressure must be applied to work for liberation of the Negro in terms of the Bill of Rights. Regardless of Byrnes's observations on his economic progress, the American Negro remains a second-class citizen. Yet Byrnes's observations also make plain how much more progress toward ending bigotry remains to be made in the self-satisfied North. Finally, they make plain how complex for each nation are the problems of this changing world. Britain and France have a long way still to go before they complete the political revolution ending what we call colonialism. But when we regard our own deficiencies, we will perhaps be more modest in denouncing those of others.

Progress has been made in our social evolution and in the imperial revolutions of Britain and France. No similar progress can yet be detected within the bleak imperial confines of the U.S.S.R. The philosophy of democracy and those freedoms it implies are still the free world's exclusive property. We should remember this even while recalling faults in its practice.

The task of asserting ourselves in the contest for other men's minds is assuredly not easy. We are perplexed by inner torments we have not yet resolved. And we cannot, without risking freedom, co-ordinate such branches of our cultural life as writing and the cinema for the mere sake of advertising national virtue. Above all, the race issue, so important in a world containing a majority of colored nations, is an Achilles' heel in all our propaganda efforts. It will remain so until we cure the ailment that still plagues us. Our voice must echo with embarrassment abroad till democracy applies to citizens of every pigmentation.

But surely, if we confine ourselves to temperate and honest presentation of our aims and intentions, describing what we seek to accomplish in achieving our ideals, refraining from the temptation to stress other countries' faults, we will increase the respect, if not the liking, entertained for us. It is not probable that we shall ever be loved by many weaker lands; nor is this even desirable. As I have written earlier, charity rarely inspires love. Anyway, a craving for popularity is naïve. What we should above all covet is respect.

Propaganda is an important aspect of policy and a curious element of political warfare. Perhaps it can only be dynamically successful under a dictatorship and when postulated on the Big Lie, as in Nazi Germany or Soviet Russia, both adepts in this field. We can never, and must never, compete in such a contest.

And if we are not, like our adversaries, in the lie business, we must improve the reality of that image our propagandists reflect abroad. Furthermore, we must ask our leaders, before making hasty pronouncements useful for internal purposes, to reflect on how these statements may be interpreted overseas.

Propaganda has to deal with policy as expressed, or misexpressed, by a nation's outstanding men. A glib jingo phrase by a bellicose admiral or general or a hasty quip by a cabinet minister can undo weeks of careful overseas broadcasting. It would be useful if our propaganda would recognize that most of this world is politically neither black nor white. Ideological hectoring can be offensive and unrealistic. We happily condemn fascism and Communism, yet ally ourselves to Franco and bolster Tito. Perhaps someday we may even improve relationships with a Poland that continues to call itself a Communist state. What our policy and propaganda should oppose is not ideology but imperialism, menace, and expansion.

We should cease smug criticisms of "colonialism"—a varying system that is by no means always bad. Not only is such carping offensive to certain of our allies, but it might be considered bad taste in a nation that itself continues to control areas as distant as Okinawa. And we must, above all, take scrupulous pains to co-ordinate advice to subject peoples with our policy intentions toward those same peoples. Prior to the Hungarian revolt, the populations of Eastern Europe relied—on the basis of American radio programs—upon United States assistance if they ever dared rebel against Moscow. It was not only deceitful, cruel, and immoral to permit such an impression to be conveyed, even by implication, but ultimately it did serious damage to our cause.

If we but adhere to calm truth in the pronouncements of our statesmen and of our official channels of communication; if we discuss our own faults frankly while avoiding preachments to others; and if we stress and restress our ideals rather than the extent of our wealth and comfort, we shall earn the esteem and confidence of foreigners.

That, after all, is what our propaganda should aspire to: a demonstration that we truly are *superior* to our enemies.

Chapter 4

Some Weaknesses in Approach

A foreign policy is as necessary to a nation as a code of behavior is to an individual. It governs the pattern of relationships of one nation to another.

United States foreign policy is the sum total of aspirations and reactions of the American people with regard to the other peoples of the world. It is not static. It changes with the changing aspirations and reactions of our citizens, which are channeled through the legislative and executive branches of the government.

Even under so dominating a secretary of state as John Foster Dulles, our foreign policy is not the conscious decision of a single man or group of men. It is fluent. As we and other nations change our hopes, our intentions, and our physical circumstances, our foreign policy also changes.

Our relationships with Germany, Italy, Japan, and Russia during the past two decades reveal clearly how much we change. It is perfectly possible to imagine that a decade or two hence we might be great friends with Moscow, allied against a Peiping-Tokyo axis, or vice versa. The pattern of policy as it is applied shifts constantly.

The basic objective of American foreign policy does not alter. We seek to create a stable, orderly, and peaceful world, one in which all countries, particularly our own, make a special contribution to prosperity and international harmony. For more than a decade, operating in differing ways as scientific and political revolutions continue to modify the global balance, we have pursued a fairly continuous set of short-term and long-term objectives.

The former may be defined accordingly: (1) to prove to the U.S.S.R. and its allies that it is unwise and unprofitable to attempt to overrun the Eurasian land mass; (2) by inducing restraint upon the more dynamic Communist states, to persuade them to accept real peace treaties guaranteeing international stability.

The latter could also be described in simple terms: (1) to achieve better understanding abroad of what the United States is and desires to be; (2) to make our own special talents and wealth available overseas on terms that are fair to both the American and foreign nations; (3) to facilitate an improvement in the present imbalance in international economic relationships; (4) to try to tranquilize the political climate sufficiently to reduce the burden of an armaments race and increase the efficiency of the United Nations.

I venture to say that the most ardent Democrat and the most ardent Republican would concur with this statement of broad objectives. Only in the application of policy would there be sharp disagreement, for diplomacy, which seeks to attain policy goals, is necessarily fluid in a fluid world.

Furthermore, as Platonic philosophy argues, objectives (such as "perfection," shall we say) cannot be attained, only approached. Some problems can never be *permanently* solved. And these we must learn to live with. Nor can we even fix advance dates by which more limited goals must or should be reached.

The difficulties confronting those currently charged with the direction of our foreign policy are extensive and complex. There are geographical relationships with the nations of each continent. There are political and military relationships. There are economic, racial, ideological, and scientific relationships. It is impossible in a book of this scope and nature to even begin to analyze each of these sectors. I do not propose, for example, to deal at all with our harmonious relationships with such lands as Canada, Australia, and New Zealand; to delve into the extraordinary maze of relationships with Latin America; to scrutinize the problems shaping up in Black Africa. Nor, in this chapter, will I deal at any length with NATO or with the very special problems of the Far East, which relate directly to China, or the Middle East.

The essential challenge at this moment in history is that of our contest with the Sino-Soviet bloc, spearhead of a new and dynamic imperialist movement. This, like the Arab invasions of the seventh century, is at the same time political, military, and ideological.

As Moscow and Washington eye each other nervously, both appear to be experiencing broadly similar changes within their governing systems. One can detect a certain parallelism as each superpower strives to improve its efficiency to meet competitive threats from the other.

In Russia this is shown in several striking tendencies, all intended to decentralize a government that has become too cumbersome to handle the problems of an increasingly intricate modern society. In 1957 Khrushchev began this process by starting to deconcentrate industrial controls. He wants to break up Communism's behemoth trusts into a series of smaller organizations throughout the country, not centered in Moscow. At the same time, he seeks to localize the system of collecting those turnover taxes upon which Soviet financing depends. He wishes to introduce the same philosophy to farming. By abolishing state-owned machine tractor stations and turning their machinery over to the *kholkhozes,* he hopes to make the latter more independent-minded and therefore more productive.

The Khrushchev "evolution," which, like everything in Russia, is instigated from the top, has met with opposition from Communist conservatives. The result has been, perhaps paradoxically, to force assumption of more dictatorial powers to sweep out opponents while trying to reduce dictatorship, or at least to parcel out responsibilities. But Khrushchev has never relinquished control over the police and army. For some years after Lavrenti P. Beria's execution, General Ivan A. Serov remained quietly, anonymously, but efficiently at the party bosses' total disposition. By placing his security forces at their orders, he helped remove from the military their symbol of independence, Marshal Georgi Zhukov. Now, having accomplished this task, Serov has been quietly, anonymously, but efficiently ousted.

It may seem odd that, just as Khrushchev attempts to loosen up the Soviet totalitarian system, the United States should be asking greater intrusion of Washington into many aspects of national life. By contrast with Russia, this movement derives from public opinion and not from the government itself. There is growing demand that we rid ourselves of traditional prejudices against a compact general staff and really unify our sprawling defense apparatus. New voices also insist that it is folly to devise programs financially on a basis of annual appropriations when competing internationally with five-year Soviet planning. Many intelligent people talk of the desirability of legislating for longer-range expenditure schedules in several fields. One also hears suggestions that civilian specialists should be placed temporarily at federal disposal or subjected to some form of conscripted service.

Comparison between this groping for more efficiency in America and in Russia is striking. There is a remarkable coincidence between these movements, and a contrast in goals and methods. Max Lerner recently observed: "Both of us worship magnitudes, both stress success, both respect material results, both think in technical terms, both make a fetish of engineering, both have elevated managerial men to the top (in America we call him the businessman, in Russia he is the commissar who heads a Government trust), both are organizing a mass-society—and both are in danger of being destroyed and destroying each other."

This dual destiny of today's superpowers was long ago sensed by Tocqueville. In the early nineteenth century he wrote: "There are, at the present time, two great nations in the world which seem to tend toward the same end, although they started from different points. I allude to the Russians and the Americans. . . . The American relies upon personal interest to accomplish his ends and gives free scope to the unguided exertions and common sense of the citizens. The Russian centers all the authority of society in a single arm. The principal instrument of the former is freedom, of the latter servitude."

Tocqueville saw that complete liberty might have to be voluntarily curbed. He said: "I have no hesitation in predicting that if the people of the United States is ever involved in serious difficulties, its taxation will speedily be increased." This trend toward restriction has been visible for decades. The income tax, once resented as an intrusion on personal liberty, is an assumed fact of life. So are federal aid to education and supervision over interstate commerce, transport, and other modern social complexities.

The movement toward greater control by our central government seems fated to continue. Only by extending national responsibility can we gear ourselves to competitive coexistence in a shrinking world. But Moscow, in contrast, must break up its overcentralized, top-heavy machine. Otherwise its system may freeze into outmoded immobility. The philosophical comparison is intriguing. Americans, while recognizing the need for adjustment to a terrible challenge, fear the grant of too much power to their chosen rulers. Khrushchev's problem is posed from an opposite pole. He obviously worries about giving too much power to the people. But both nations are attempting to bring to bear in world relationships the consequences of this dual search for efficiency.

Each has likewise realized the importance to foreign policy of economic aid to other nations. This was most signally expressed in the United States by what became known as the Marshall Plan. The Marshall Plan represented a far more profound development in our thinking than was at first apparent. Even isolationist politicians have come to accept—since Secretary of State Marshall's famous Harvard speech, June 5, 1947—the idea that it can be in our own interest to contribute aid to friendly nations overseas.

Unfortunately, however, the wisdom displayed in the Marshall Plan was not equally apparent in policy attitudes elsewhere in the world. In Western Europe we shrewdly set the regional economy on its feet before installing upon this base the necessary burden of a military alliance. All too often, in other areas, we have acted precisely in the reverse.

Thus, we have either fostered or joined military pacts in the Middle East, Southeast Asia, and the Orient that did not have the initial foundation of economic health. The result has been, in certain instances, to create a debilitating rather than a strengthening factor. Some poor nations have found themselves saddled with the permanent burden of keeping up a modern defense apparatus which their industrial and fiscal structure is incapable of supporting. The result is a tendency toward internal weakness, vitiating the value of an army.

During the years that followed the Marshall Plan and the creation of NATO, our policy experienced a form of pactomania. Weapons overbalanced welfare. This phase has, to a considerable degree, now been righted. But we have not yet been able to bring about the necessary nonmilitary programs in free Asia or burgeoning Africa.

It is, of course, impossible to dream of ever accomplishing on those continents the same kind of success that we achieved

in Europe with the Marshall Plan. Europe is a dynamic, industrialized, highly educated region. It has a vast reservoir of
technical skills that cannot be approached in underdeveloped
areas. Furthermore, the countries joined in the Organization
for European Economic Cooperation have a very considerable common political heritage. This does not exist elsewhere.

It is time to return to the original philosophy expressed in
the Marshall Plan. We must help our friends abroad. And it is
wiser to help them first in economic ways. For example, there
is no point in continuing to increase our military assistance to
Pakistan. If we could freeze it at its present level and invest
more funds in productive fields, we might do more to shore up
that courageous but impoverished land. If the emphasis of
our Asian policy is thus adjusted, we will find ourselves on better terms with neutralist nations—above all, India. And this
is vitally important.

It is in what President Eisenhower terms our own "enlightened self-interest" to see the free world strong. The free
world includes many uncommitted nations as well as those
aligned with us as loyal partners. We have now devoted much
energy and money to the bolstering of foreign military defenses. It is time to pay more attention to the economic structure upon which liberty must in the end rely.

The fact that foreigners do not vote makes many of our
legislators regard aid bills with gingerly distaste. Appropriations to build a dam in Africa or Asia have scant ballot-box
appeal. Nevertheless, Congress must be persuaded of the *permanent* need to sustain massive assistance programs abroad.
James H. Smith, Jr., head of the International Cooperation
Administration, says: "One thing we are not trying to do and
should not try to do is to buy friends with this program. You
cannot buy friends with a program of economic assistance. We
are trying to strengthen the economies of this uncommitted
area of the world so they can be independent of any foreign

domination including even the domination of the United States itself."

This is a worthy objective. It is consonant with our traditional policy. We consider that only a nation internally strong can be free. Such freedom does not depend upon alliance with ourselves. We respect neutrality, despite occasional confused homilies by our statesmen. The Marshall Plan had no initial military significance. Yet, when NATO developed out of it because of Soviet pugnacity, one of its principal members was neutral Turkey. Sweden and Switzerland, habitual neutrals, joined the O.E.E.C., which grew from the Marshall Plan.

If some fledgling countries do not receive outside succor, they face economic disintegration. And in most of them there exists only one well-organized political minority prepared to exploit resulting chaos. This is the Communist party. Therefore, logic dictates American assistance.

There is also a philosophical argument in favor of foreign aid. A strong evangelical tradition has influenced American thinking since Colonial days. This considers it a disgrace to permit unchallenged poverty. It is mirrored in Smith's plea that we help foreign countries the way "you would [support] a new enterprise in your own community." Smith says that this should not be "done with the finely sharpened pencil of a banker but done with a little extra measure of faith in the future and done with the intent to produce results far in excess of costs both for the United States and the recipient country." In a sense, he contends, we have much the same charitable obligation to other peoples that inspires prosperous citizens to give to their own Community Chest.

Finally, we must see that the United States, as a trading nation, depends heavily on foreign markets. The more purchasing power there is in another land, the higher its standard of living and the better competitive chance we may have to share in its commerce. Britain found this out long ago. After the Napoleonic Wars, London invested heavily on the ravaged

Continent in order to restore its business. Ernest Bevin recalled this when sponsoring our Marshall Plan.

If we refuse aid and a country turns to the Soviet bloc, we risk being squeezed out by restrictive barter agreements fixed in Moscow. And we increase the chances of war or depression if we lose our trade. The last great conflict cost the United States $360,000,000,000. Until 1952 the purely economic price of rehabilitation was $29,000,000,000. Surely it is less expensive to pay for rehabilitation first.

The reasons favoring continued and expanded foreign aid are perhaps not entirely easy to explain to the American voter. But Russia understands them. Khrushchev says: "We declare war upon the United States in the peaceful field of trade. The threat to the United States is not the ICBM, but in the field of peaceful production."

There are two essential aspects of competitive coexistence. The first is the relative rate of increase in productivity within the Western and Soviet blocs themselves. The second is the contest between these blocs for commercial and political ascendancy in uncommitted African and Asian lands.

Too often we are deluded by the success of our own fat-dripping, luxurious civilization. We started competition with innumerable advantages: incomparably high living standards, immense industrial plant, wealth, and military predominance. This edge is vanishing. The West represents a small minority in global population, but disproportionate power. That power is now fading as Russia catches up to us in great leaps.

By 1960 the U.S.S.R. plans to produce as much coal, steel, electricity, and oil as the six nations of Europe's common market. By 1965 it plans to produce as much as all Western Europe. Before 1970, if our own productivity rates are not accelerated, it hopes to forge ahead of the United States.

China boasts that by 1960 it will be making 20,000,000 tons of steel a year, as compared with Britain's 22,000,000. The Communist states have not yet translated this astonishing output into visible living comforts. But soon they will be in a position to do so if they wish.

The underdeveloped countries regard this race with rapt attention. They see the rate of Soviet productivity continuing at a ratio several times our own. They see the rate of growth in China increasing at twice that of democracy's only Asian showpiece, India.

These statistics are interpreted in many neutral capitals as gauges of the relative worth of Communism and non-Communism. And Moscow backs this with a skillful foreign-aid program that is beginning, in various places, to dim the luster of our achievements in a field we had previously considered peculiarly our own.

Soviet-bloc assistance to backward areas now approximately equals Western nonmilitary help—although it is primarily in the form of promised credits, only a fifth of which have yet been taken up. The Communists do not generally export consumer goods. Instead, they arrange to purchase raw materials and to send equipment and technicians to build factories.

Moscow has been preparing this program for years and has educated thousands of specialists in the languages and problems of foreign nations. These experts are servants of the state and cannot be drawn off by competing businesses. The West has limited cadres of its own experts. And most of them disappear into private industry, to which they are attracted by higher salaries than governments can afford to pay.

By acquiring raw materials, the Communist bloc not only deprives the West of such needed supplies but can dump them when desired in order to break world prices. By tying foreign economies to ruble exchange, it shrinks Western export markets. By fomenting scares, it frightens Western private overseas-investment schemes.

We must combat this threat on both a short-term and a long-term basis. We need to develop far more technicians, of whom the U.S.S.R. now produces twice as many as the United States. We must seek means of stabilizing prices and assuring markets for the goods of poor countries. We must help these countries to develop themselves in business partnerships on a level of equality with the West. If necessary, we must legislate ways of drafting civilian experts temporarily for peacetime service as we draft youths into the armed forces.

Our friends can help with money, men, and material. President Eisenhower pointed out one way to achieve this when he suggested an international development organization linked with the World Bank. Surely all the Allied powers must now recognize that in both internal production schedules and improvement of backward regions we must do more, and more efficiently, else we are ultimately lost.

To emphasize this point, Moscow is sponsoring an effective, well-conceived aid program of its own. It is directly competitive, adroitly administered, and has already registered important gains in a domain we had come to assume was almost wholly ours. Surely it would be folly for us to abdicate before this challenge.

In contemplating the rivalry between our own and Soviet aid programs to uncommitted nations, we must remember one salient point: despite Moscow propaganda, Russia is ruled not by a communist but by a state capitalist system. The government and not the individual worker controls all wealth, which can then be disposed of most efficiently in the national interest.

Since World War II, we have disbursed about ten times as much as the U.S.S.R. on foreign assistance of all kinds. Like Russia, we have spent huge sums to help allies militarily or to unload accumulated stocks. But we confuse defense support and purely economic help. If we send rifles to a friend, we charge our taxpayers replacement value rather than actual worth. This boosts listed costs of military support. As Moscow has done in the satellites, Egypt, and Syria, we have developed a considerable second-hand market for obsolescent weapons.

We also export immense amounts of surplus commodities under Public Law 480. These pile up at home because they cannot be sold at lower world prices, and are therefore bought by Washington. When they are delivered abroad for smaller local-currency payments, we list them at artificially high values on our books.

We must be careful not to exaggerate the relative proportion of contributions or loans for defense purposes or to help unload stocks. But even in the field of altruistic assistance for underdeveloped lands, we find we must spend much more than Moscow. There are several reasons why this is necessary for free enterprise as opposed to state capitalism.

We are openly wary of helping regimes we regard as "socialistic." Our government does not like to undercut our own businessmen. Congress stipulated that the new development fund shall not compete overseas with "private investment capital."

Our banking system pays more to borrow money at home than does Russia's. Therefore, the Treasury insists on higher interest rates for loans abroad, in order not to lose. Likewise, when we need experts to administer foreign programs we must await termination of their private contracts. We have no method of conscription for civilian work.

The luxury of freedom requires an expensive approach to foreign aid. The Russians can offer tentative loans they do not necessarily intend to fulfill. If they wish to propagandize a country and suggest help, they wait to see if we will propose a rival program. If we do not, they move in. If we do, they abstain. Thus they can operate with a smaller revolving fund. They probe our interest economically as they used to do militarily. They have suggested a $25,000,000 credit to our ally Iceland. They are shopping around in Africa in hopes of developing a sympathetic bloc.

As an autocracy, the Soviet Union has a huge pool of trained technicians. A job in Kiev or a job in New Delhi is equally a state job. No draft is needed. Foreign loans do not have to be treated in terms of financial profit. As a matter of fact, even at low interest charges such loans lose no money.

We exact from 3 to 4 per cent in dollar repayments and from 4 to 6 per cent in local currency repayments. Moscow charges from 2 to 2½ per cent because its own internal borrowing pays on this scale. This makes things easy for Russia's foreign-aid boss.

As we try to make loan conditions more favorable, the U.S.S.R. does the same. Its Indian loans no longer start repayment from date of equipment delivery. The borrower now is not charged until an enterprise built from such equipment actually starts to produce.

State capitalism permits highhanded flexibility. All this discourages Americans who feel we spend too much for too little political return. Kennan says: "Moscow is not exactly the bottomless horn of plenty. . . . It is a pity that it has never been required to respond all at once to the many expectations directed to it. We ourselves would be the last, one would think, to wish to spare it this test."

The trouble is we can neither abandon the field nor give up our workable but costly free-enterprise society. We cannot allow Russia a free hand in economic penetration. We have seen what it means in Egypt and Syria. We have moral obligations to succor poorer peoples. We have mercantile and strategic interests. We cannot permit Soviet efficiency to oust us from a field in which we long predominated.

Congress must ponder this problem. Naturally, no democratic free-enterprise system can compete in every way on equal terms with autocratic state capitalism. Therefore, in the national interest, we should agree, when needed, to relax federal banking standards and lend money at a loss. And we should make available to the administration a flexible contingency fund to use for emergency purposes not now foreseeable. We cannot plan ahead against a five-year-plan autocracy merely with annual appropriations.

Unfortunately, we do not yet devote a sufficient proportion of our wealth to that foreign economic aid necessary to encourage stability. And we do devote a disproportionately large amount to the barren program of purely military assistance.

There is little question but that we have become "pact-happy" and have overextended ourselves by promising military support for too many countries in too widely spread an area. We are, indeed, committed to defend no less than forty-five nations on five continents. This terrestrial system of alliances would have been inconceivable fifteen years ago. Nevertheless, the scope, if not the precise nature, of such pacts is an inevitable development. After all, through the United Nations, we have promised to react against aggression anywhere.

Thirty-seven of our specific military commitments were made by a Democratic administration. These include twenty Latin-American lands with whom we joined in a treaty of reciprocal assistance at Rio de Janeiro in 1947, a treaty that reaffirmed America's oldest foreign-policy tenet and put teeth into the Monroe Doctrine. Eleven NATO allies were accepted in 1949, and Greece and Turkey in 1952. In Europe, only West Germany's partnership was a Republican action.

These commitments are a logical consequence of past friendships, cold war, and fear of Soviet domination. The Democrats, aided by Mr. Dulles, before he became secretary of state, linked us with Australia, New Zealand, and then Japan by security treaties. A mutual defense accord with the Philippines was signed in 1951. Apart from Germany, all military alliances accepted by the Eisenhower administration have been in Asia. These include mutual defense treaties with South Korea and Nationalist China as well as the Southeast Asia Treaty Organization pact, which commits us to defend Pakistan, Thailand, Laos, Cambodia, and South Vietnam.

We have special arrangements for bases in exchange for self-defense assistance with several allied nations and also with Spain, Libya, Ethiopia, and Saudi Arabia. But these are not technically alliances. We lend moral support to the faltering Balkan pact, including Yugoslavia, and to the Northern Tier, including Iran, Turkey, Pakistan, as well as Britain. Iraq's membership is now lapsing.

Only in Asia have we evolved brand-new policy conceptions. The retreat of colonial empires and the simultaneous advance of Communism forced us to bolster Japan, the Philippines, Australia, and New Zealand. The Korean war prompted guarantees for South Korea and Formosa.

Regional pacts are most awkward in the vast expanse between the Philippines and the Mediterranean—SEATO, of which we are a member, and the Northern Tier and Balkan alliances, which we indirectly backstop. SEATO involves us in a difficult commitment to prevent conquest of Southeast Asia by indirect aggression. But Indochina is wobbly; Thailand hints at a growth of neutralism; and Pakistan is restless. The Northern Tier has never demonstrated vigor. Previously, a similar arrangement—the Saadabad pact—failed to create a real alliance in the same area. The Balkan pact displays many of the weaknesses that destroyed its predecessor, the Balkan Entente.

After World War I, France, then a great power, devised a series of alliances in Eastern Europe with the idea of containing Germany. But the French were unable to give economic backing to the countries involved. Germany gobbled up their foreign trade and thereby weakened political and military ties.

We should learn from the unsuccessful French experience that, first of all, it is necessary to harmonize the interests of our friends. If not, quarrels between South Korea and Japan or Greece and Turkey could wreck any over-all defensive system. Already these arguments resemble the fatal dispute between Poland and Czechoslovakia that began the disruption of Paris's prewar coalition.

Secondly, we ought to realize from France's failure the need to support military commitments with economic aid and commercial opportunities. We did, indeed, move successfully with NATO, where we built an economic foundation through the Marshall Plan before we dressed it in uniform. In a less-organized way we have shored up sagging Latin-American economies and assisted many Asian nations.

But we still lack a co-ordinated economic program in the East. It is no longer desirable to extend military commitments there. Instead, it is necessary to help Asian economic planning on a massive scale. Only thus can we hope to prevent Soviet commercial intrusion, with inevitable political consequences.

Our proclaimed aim is to strengthen all the free world, but we have not yet shown complete willingness to accept the logical consequences of this policy. If we fail to rectify this lack, we would justifiably be subject to the charge of pactomania, because in such a case, the pacts we so carefully developed would remain incomplete and weak. They were erected against war. But this is an era of competitive coexistence.

We should furthermore consider the philosophical implications of our intricate alliance structure. It is based on political rather than ideological realities. It does not, in any sense, bind us only with democratic powers. When we make pompous preachments on the subject of abstract freedom we might do well first to consider what we have come to represent as leader of a massive set of coalitions.

In one of those occasional frank conversations now permitted the Russians, a well-placed Soviet Communist complained to me two years ago: "American foreign policy is too rigid. You struggle to prevent historically inevitable changes. You seek to encircle us with a holy alliance intended to preserve regimes already demonstrably outmoded—merely to check Communism's spread."

There is a kernel of truth in this observation. Our network of military pacts—some multilateral like NATO and SEATO, some bilateral like base arrangements with Saudi Arabia and Spain—often strengthens governmental systems we ourselves find distasteful. Few would argue that Jeffersonian principles are advanced by bolstering Franco's despotism, the dictatorships of Chiang Kai-shek and Syngman Rhee, or King Saud's slave-owning absolutism.

However, the Russian's critique is an instance of the pot calling the kettle black. As Moscow proved so convincingly in Hungary, it is the Soviet pact system that is in reality today's holy alliance. No member dares change its ideology or allegiance—regardless of how unpopular these become with government or people.

Evidently Washington links itself with other capitals on a basis of strategic convenience rather than political preference. This may be embarrassing to doctrinal purists. But, as history has proven, it is the only logical basis for alliance. It happens that in Europe we have military ties with several truly democratic nations. But certain ideologically sympathetic lands like Switzerland and Sweden, for reasons of their own, remain unaligned. And such allied powers as Turkey and Portugal could hardly be called democracies. In Asia the problem becomes still more difficult. Only two really democratic governments exist between Greece and Japan—Israel and India. Yet the former cannot practicably be brought into our defensive scheme until its relationships with the Arab bloc are pacified. And the latter chooses to follow a strictly neutral path.

Undoubtedly, we and our stronger Western allies try to favor political evolution where possible in backward portions of the world. This may take such distressingly limited forms as London's authorization of its officials to manumit slaves escaping from Saudi Arabia (some two dozen were thus freed in 1956 in Persian Gulf consulates). Or it may assume the shape of mild pressure for democratic tenets in underdeveloped countries.

Such persuasions must inevitably be adjusted to prevailing circumstance. For instance, it has become clear in Indonesia that democracy has yet to meet the test of governing capacity. And in Iraq, Pakistan, and Burma, generals have imposed personal rule.

Until World War II and our alliance of convenience with the U.S.S.R., we generally sought (outside of Latin America) to bind ourselves militarily with ideologically sympathetic governments. Now, in assuming the burden of world power, we discover that not many such governments exist.

Upon scrutiny it becomes apparent that ours is indeed a very unholy alliance. It is founded on nondoctrinaire assumptions: that independent lands should not be swallowed by a Communism which permits no later escape; and that essential interests of our own and allied nations must be safeguarded. The obverse of the coin is the restrictive Sino-Soviet system of military plus ideological pacts.

The original holy alliance of post-Napoleonic Europe was, it may be noted, the product of a Russian mind. Czar Alexander I deliberately linked ideology, in the form of religion and royalty, with political strategy. He sought to perpetuate existing frontiers and regimes in the name, not of popular desire, but of ruling sovereigns, and to bind peoples as "members of one and the same Christian nation."

Modern Russia's coalition philosophically resembles this conception except that it substitutes the word "Communist" for "Christian." Furthermore, it seeks not only to retain that which is already committed ideologically and militarily to Moscow's direction; it aims to expand outward.

America's defensive scheme includes several partners evidently not of our ideological choice. But we appear to have learned from that great statesman Richelieu, who taught that the interest of the state was primary and eternal, and above sentimental, ideological, or doctrinal prejudices. If national interest demanded an alliance with an obnoxious government, then no feelings should be permitted to blur that necessity. In moments of danger one should choose one's allies, not for charm, but for physical or geographical value.

The objective of our curious assortment of pacts is dual. The obvious aim is to contain Sino-Soviet expansion. The less obvious aim is to make possible that dream of United States diplomacy, the freeing from Communist control of the areas it dominates. But right now the problem is not yet how to apply such politically popular but practically meaningless slogans as "roll back." Right now the question is not how to shrink the immense Sino-Soviet empire. The immediate requirement is to prevent still other nations from slipping into our opponent's fold.

The Communist area where we reckon there exists the best chance of future change favorable to our concepts is that of Eastern Europe. Already this has been explosively marked by discontent and revolt in East Germany, Poland, and Hungary. But neither in application nor in announced purpose has our policy yet sufficiently adjusted to new realities and potential opportunities in the area between the Black Sea and the Baltic. We continue to delude both ourselves and our friends with pat slogans. Madison Avenue salesmanship techniques are an inadequate substitute for wisdom.

Such phrases as "liberation" are politically popular in the United States and ideally to be desired. But this is not an ideal world. Under prevailing conditions, the satellite states are not going to alter their form of government because of any diplomatic methods we apply. These changes must be prised out of Moscow by the satellites themselves.

Revolution is not a static thing, as events in Poland have proven. The situation need not remain static. Already the reign of terror appears to be lessening. Whenever Moscow begins to ease the tightness of its controlling reins, it is up to us to exploit differences, divergent interests, and cravings among the Eastern peoples. But we are not doing this enough; we still insist upon regarding most of the puppet countries as a single group despite their evident dissimilarities.

As I have written in a previous book, *The Big Thaw* (Harper, 1956): "There are only two feasible ways of liberating countries within the Soviet orbit. One is by force. The other is by aiding them to gradually extricate themselves. History has tested both methods. Communist Hungary, in 1919, was freed by Allied intervention employing Rumanian troops. Titoist Yugoslavia, while retaining its ideology, broke away from Soviet control in 1948 without a war." (And Poland has moved part way in this direction.)

"When Secretary Dulles took charge of the State Department in 1953, his talk of 'liberation' implied that the United States was prepared to support with force if necessary any counter-revolutions in East Europe. But later that year an uprising in East Germany proved this implication wrong. The Western World, led by ourselves, sat back and watched the insurrection being crushed. This was a lesson to the satellites." (It was grimly and dramatically repeated in Hungary.)

"Nevertheless, discontented populations continued to believe that some day war might come, a war that ultimately would change their governmental systems. Added credence was given by public utterances of some of our statesmen and by torrents of propaganda from our radio stations, many of them manned by emigres from communism, dreaming tragically of their return. This thought, too, faded after the Geneva summit conference. Whatever else that meeting may or may not have accomplished, it convinced Europe that war was out as a form of political disagreement. . . .

"What, we must ask ourselves, is the aim of our policy? What proportion of it is founded upon selfish aspirations such as weakening our enemy's strength and what on altruism?

How much are we thinking of aiding East Europe in terms of improving our own global position and how much are we thinking of aiding the people who live there?

"The greatest fault of our satellite policy, both as announced and as applied, is that it has not concentrated upon the attainable. It has persistently worked for what is patently impossible except in the event of the war that we ourselves rule out.

"The existence of Titoism is to an extent a consequence of United States foreign policy. That is to say, without our political support, military assistance and economic aid, it is unlikely that Yugoslavia would have managed to survive its quarrel with Moscow and the Cominform blockade.

"What Titoism means to the subjected satellite populations is not escape from existing Communist forms. Rather it signifies development of national independence and easier contact with the West. It implies liberty of political as distinct from ideological action. And even if Yugoslavia should ever rejoin the Soviet orbit this abstract concept of Titoism will remain. The idea of Protestantism would have continued even if Luther and Calvin had recanted.

"Plainly we must practice different forms of foreign policy toward captive states and toward free states, of which there are not yet any in Moscow's sphere" (not even excepting Poland). "With regard to the former the primary objective is to release them from foreign control. In this respect our initial aims in Eastern Europe coincide with those proclaimed by Tito.

"Our aspiration is to split the U.S.S.R.'s European empire into individual segments. Even if each retains its present ideology, nothing in terms of ultimate goals is sacrificed by such procedure. The United States will be no less popular or influential with the masses of independent Communist nations than it now is with the masses of subjected Communist nations. That is demonstrable in Yugoslavia.

"It is not the task of United States foreign policy to oppose communism as an ideology. Our tradition is to allow any country to choose its own form of government. What we oppose is enslavement by outside powers. Legitimately we cannot object to communism as such. But we can and do object to Soviet imperialism. . . .

"Our ultimate hope is that captive peoples may some day be able to choose the governments they desire as promised at Yalta. But this is not presently attainable. Our initial goal is to loosen the bloc. Even in this restricted sense there are foreseeable diplomatic consequences.

"Tito pretends to neutralism, an 'active neutralism' separated from either power coalition. Until now neutralism has been moving outward from Moscow like ripples from a stone dropped in the Soviet pond. Let us seek to reverse the trend. Lord knows the satellite populations long to be freed from their present ties. We cannot expect subservient governments to scrap the Warsaw Pact. But we can attempt to prepare for Eastern Europe new political positions from which, some day, they might venture demands for withdrawal of Soviet missions and troops. . . ."

Washington quietly adapted some of these ideas after the dramatic 1956 explosions in Hungary and Poland. Certainly the United States has behaved with wisdom and restraint both in official and unofficial relations with Warsaw since the advent of the Gomulka government. It is not our fault that Gomulka has been forced part way back into a Soviet prison and that we have therefore had to ration our generous impulses. But we must be prepared always to move flexibly in the potentially profitable field of satellite Europe. We tend to ignore the historical and national aspirations of such peoples as the Czechs and Romanians when we contemplate the role of their countries. We have not even yet bothered to re-establish relationships with Bulgaria, a rather obdurately supine Soviet puppet, since they were broken off in 1950. Yet Sofia has made many efforts to restore diplomatic contacts. This is a matter of little internal political import within the United States, unlike the recognition of Red China. Why in Heaven's name do we not again exchange missions? At least that would afford the unhappy Bulgars an indication that we are interested in their fate. And whatever we learned from that interesting Balkan listening post might help to fill in many missing pieces of the obscure Communist picture puzzle.

Finally, in the realm of Eastern Europe, we must not forget the eventual possibility that the second way of working to liberate the area from Moscow—aiding enslaved lands gradually to extricate themselves—may someday become possible under the theory of what is now popularly called "disengagement." Proposals to this end have been made by Poland's foreign minister, Rapacki, Hugh Gaitskell of the British Labor party, and George Kennan. For various reasons, none of these formulas has yet been presented in an acceptable fashion. But the thought remains very much alive on both sides of the Iron Curtain.

The other frontier of the Sino-Soviet empire, in Asia, is far more difficult for us to penetrate, for, in that region, as I have written, history appears to be on the Communist side. Where Communism has moved southward or eastward into Asia, broadly speaking it has represented a modern trend. While there are exceptions to this proposition, it can be argued that the essential logic is correct.

Resentments against Russia have been intensified by declining social levels in areas like the Baltic states, incorporated into the U.S.S.R., or in communized countries such as Hungary, Poland, and Czechoslovakia. This creates a situation in Europe inherently favorable to the West. As a long-term factor aiding the liberating processes of history, it helped push the Iron Curtain eastward out of Austria.

The Russians themselves, being expert in geopolitics, probably took this situation into account in postwar planning. Stalin implied to Harold Stassen that he would not tolerate in any neighbor a living standard higher than that existing in the U.S.S.R. The Soviet expansion plan foresaw its westernmost limit along a Trieste-Stettin line with Greece excepted. But Yugoslavia, Trieste, and now East Austria have escaped the orbit. The historical tide runs with us in Europe.

But such is not the case in Asia. Both before and after the Russian Revolution, where Russia expanded southward and eastward it brought more, rather than less, civilization. Methods employed were often brutal. But ultimately, living and educational conditions improved for various Central Asian and Siberian peoples. This trend has been accentuated by the ideological conquest of China. A vast new force, still gathering strength, has been added to Communism's Asian momentum.

Far more than military power, a combination of economic and psychological attractions threatens to crumble those portions of Southeast and South Asia that we consider necessary to keep free. The U.S.S.R. maintains negligible military forces in Central Asia. And the Chinese Communist regime has scarcely any units in the South. At this time the threat to Southeast Asia is not an armed threat.

The essential problem is recognized in the administration's program of assistance for free Asia. This envisions an eight-year plan for technical and economic aid. The ultimate goal is to raise the gross national product of backward peoples by as much as 30 per cent. One may only hope that ultimately free Asia is prepared to take the initiative in any regional program to use our economic aid.

There is great food deficiency in the area, which cannot be solved merely by exporting American surpluses. India alone could annually devour our excess grain. There is massive need for technical instruction, dams, roads, factories. To many Asians, Russia has been the outstanding example of rapid industrial development. Our Point Four program has proven an inadequate counterweight. There is no cheap answer to the problem.

That we should seek to help Asia comes within the realm of what President Eisenhower terms "enlightened self-interest." It is no business deal. Canada's Lester Pearson warns against any "false idea that we can or should purchase allies." But by making capital available, we can insure Asia's ability to stand alone.

The capital we furnish is in money, technical assistance, and specific resources for immediate translation into living standards. To this the capital of Communism can add manpower. The Communists spend men for railways, roads, mines, and fabricated equipment, just as they spent men recklessly at Dienbienphu. By this crude conversion of energy into capital results, the Russians have impressed the peoples of Asia.

Washington has regarded its Asian policy as both a "holding" and a "bridging" operation. We are still in the first phase. And in carrying it out, we cannot afford to criticize all those who entertain different political theories. India, for example, may prove of great use in the process of giving real independence to backward areas of Asia. Cambodia and Burma have officially adopted India's "neutralism."

Apart from specifically geographical or regional aspects of our policy, this age of scientific and political improvisation faces us with new types of diplomatic problems. For example, we have been forced to tie our global obligations, which might well be overextended, to novel strategic concepts.

If we are to oppose direct aggression throughout the world, there is no doubt that the most economic means of doing so is by the Radford-Dulles theory of massive retaliation based upon the concept of "a bigger bang for a buck." The trouble with this approach, so eminently logical from a fiscal point of view, is that it would commit us by implication to big wars for small issues as well as for vital ones.

Likewise, ever since the Stalinist coup in Czechoslovakia in 1948, we have been toying with means of thwarting indirect aggression. This is a menace difficult to oppose. Curiously, the first man to acknowledge diplomatically the Fifth Column threat and to propose means of countering it in treaty language was an expert on the subject, Vyacheslav M. Molotov.

During the summer of 1939, Britain and France sought a Soviet alliance against Germany. The project fell through when Hitler offered Stalin a better deal. Nevertheless, during the Anglo-French negotiations, Molotov proposed a treaty article obligating the three powers to help each other in the event of Nazi "aggression, direct or *indirect* . . . against any European state." In a suggested annex Molotov specified the pact would apply in the case of "internal coup d'état or a political change favorable to the aggressor."

We have recognized the dangers of indirect aggression and have resolved to prevent it if possible. But the only effective defense now planned would appear to be the threat of total war. And this, because of the total terror it implies to us as well as any enemy, may prove inoperable.

Against either indirect aggression or limited aggression, we remain in a poor position to attempt riposte despite the enormous extent of our global commitments. We have, indeed, managed to get away with limited operations to date, such as the dispatch of troops to Lebanon. But this did not directly involve a major power such as Russia. What alternative to total war would we have should Moscow ever dare to fly "volunteer" Moslem formations to aid some Middle Eastern client?

Were United States carrier-borne aircraft to interdict Russian units en route, surely we would have to be prepared for the sharpest kind of reaction. And yet, apart from such interdiction, is there any other potential reply within the area affected? We have too small a conventional army to help contain Soviet "volunteers" on the ground without denuding our defenses elsewhere.

It is doubtful, judging from such information as we possess, that the U.S.S.R. wishes or is indeed ready to risk nuclear conflict. But this is a gamble, *in extremis,* which our present military posture forces us to accept, for we are badly prepared to fight a limited war.

The United States has a powerful navy and air force capable of devastating retaliatory striking power—the concept of our present defensive strategy. But we have only fifteen army divisions. Therefore, it is hard to conceive of our conducting a Korean-type operation again except under unusual geographical circumstances.

The Soviet Union, on the other hand, is capable of two kinds of warfare. It has geared its immense military machine to the horrible possibility of total nuclear war. But it is even better prepared to carry on old-fashioned, nonatomic conflicts, as in Hungary.

Moscow maintains a constant strength of 175 divisions, including sixty-five armored divisions. True, Russian rifle divisions are smaller than our own, but their initial firepower is nearly as heavy. The U.S.S.R.'s human reservoir is huge. In 1945 the Soviet battle order numbered 692 divisions, plus 129 air divisions. In any atomic conflict, with aircraft bombing troop concentrations, Moscow could afford to lose five divisions to every one of NATO and still replace them rapidly. And China's manpower pool is incalculable.

Despite Moscow's clever propaganda about force reductions, conscription continues at a rate unimagined in democracies. Military training is a duty for all citizens between sixteen and fifty, and reserves are called up regularly for refresher training. The Soviet Navy, although relatively weak in surface ships, has more submarines than all the rest of the world. One of Russia's technicians, Major General Olisov, observed: "Of all vessels the submarine best withstands the pressures created" by atomic war. The air force is vast—possibly 25,000 planes. The Long Range Air Force (A.D.D.), of which we know little, is directly under the defense minister. And we know the Russians lead us in the crucial field of missiles.

It would be a mistake to assume we are decisively superior in military hardware. The late German Field Marshal Heinz Guderian warned: "Nothing would be worse than to underrate the strength of a great nation as full of life as the Russian." That great eighteenth-century general Suvorov taught: "The more comfort, the less bravery." This revolutionary generation has been hardened to destruction.

Soviet intelligence is expert. Moscow newspapers printed a faked dispatch October 26, 1956, warning that Britain and France had agreed to intervene in Egypt. Five days later they did. Apparently Washington had no advance information.

We cannot assume our nuclear leadership is preponderantly decisive. If Moscow has sufficient atomic weapons to knock out industrial cores by surprise, a larger allied stock might lose its value.

Suvorov, still the classical guide for Russian strategy, advocated "Quick grasp, speed, shock." Marshal Rotmistrov of the armored forces wrote openly of the "growing role of surprise attack." The army organ, *Kraznaya Zviezda,* recently stressed the importance of "getting in the first blow."

Is it not time again to assay these facts? Does it not appear absurd that the Western coalition, with a population of perhaps 400,000,000, cannot maintain in Europe more than a tenth of the Soviet and satellite divisions facing them?

No civilian can hope to measure the factors that help our administration to decide military posture. Moscow, should it so desire, has two military choices: limited war with overpowering conventional forces, or that nuclear holocaust the whole world fears. We have little ultimate alternative but to risk the latter.

Perhaps this is correct. Perhaps civilization has exploded to such a degree with the advance of scientific knowledge that it is no longer worth relying on any reckoning but peace or victorious suicide. Current events should make us again reflect whether such is indeed the case.

The U.S.S.R., for a time, publicly forswore continuation of nuclear-weapons testing. The propaganda implications of this maneuver were evident—while it endured. At the moment, only the United States and Russia have a balanced arsenal of atomic arms. Britain is a junior member of this club. France is on the verge of joining. West Germany apparently will not long lag behind.

The industrial system of the NATO world is in a far better position to begin producing the hideous weapons of our age than is the industrial system of the Soviet bloc. France, Germany, Italy, Belgium, and such sympathetic if nonallied lands as Sweden and Switzerland are approaching a capability of nuclear fabrication. Were they all to get into the atomic business, the vast lead of the U.S.S.R., in terms of manpower and conventional military force, would begin to fade. The only way in which a Communist edge could be maintained would be by encouraging such nations as China, Poland, Czechoslovakia, and Hungary to start nuclear fabrication. But this involves an immense political risk. Moscow is apparently not anxious to push China into the atomic club. Nor do the Chinese yet have an adequate manufacturing and financial base. Moscow is even less eager to see such unsteady associates as Poland and Hungary armed with superweapons. But the United States has no allies so unsteady and so untrustworthy as are Moscow's satellites Hungary and Poland.

General Paul Gerardot, former French Air Chief of Staff, explained in the Paris *Revue Militaire Generale*: "Atomic and thermonuclear weapons undoubtedly revolutionize defense against an enemy, and it is a defense much easier to accomplish than by conventional means." This form of protection is in the end cheaper to maintain than the almost impossible burden of large mechanized armies. But to assure themselves of its umbrella, our allies wish to emulate Britain in building their own atomic warhead stockpiles so as to be independent of our Congress.

A trend toward such military thinking was evident in Europe prior to Russia's temporary ban on tests. The principal NATO powers were already putting their defensive eggs in a nuclear-missile basket. The United States had pared its Seventh Army in Germany from 200,000 to 150,000 men and trimmed its tactical air force—making up the difference with atomic arms. The British have withdrawn fifteen fighter squadrons and cut their German ground strength drastically—while building up nuclear stockpiles. The French, having pulled out the bulk of their divisions from Europe to Algeria, are making an intense effort to develop their own thermonuclear arsenal.

This is desperately unpleasant to contemplate. But it is even more unpleasant when viewed from east of the Iron Curtain. Henry A. Kissinger, an expert on this subject, points out: "Our NATO allies should have every incentive to help develop a strategy which does not force the United States to have to choose between all-out war and inaction in the defense of Europe. Rather than consider the American offer of missiles as designed for our exclusive benefit, our European allies should understand that it represents the only means by which Europe can gain a degree of influence over its future. A strong military establishment within Europe and under European control is more than ever essential."

To establish such control, Europe must have its own nuclear warheads, not American ones rationed by our Congress. But if there is to be no more testing, France, West Germany, and other NATO powers cannot ever make such weapons. Khrushchev obviously understands this. And he can afford to press the point because he knows he cannot permit his own resentful allies to start atomic production. We do not want continued and unlimited nuclear tests. But, to help end them, we shall have to amend our laws and make atomic arms available to eligible partners.

Apart from the intricate problem of arriving at a policy on nuclear weapons vis-à-vis both our enemies and our allies, we now face issues produced by the space age of sputniks and moon rockets for which we have not yet devised a national attitude. We cannot afford to wait. The current technical revolution is exploding so swiftly that man's limited political and social abilities fall steadily behind in the race with scientific achievement.

There is not even agreement on the extent of territorial waters claimed by seaside nations. This in itself is an ancient problem. For years there have been disputes between countries arguing for a three-mile limit and those contending that twelve miles is a fair minimum. The question was infinitely complicated when Chile, Peru, and Ecuador insisted on controlling fishing 200 miles out.

It seems odd that this simple puzzle has not been settled when the world is already talking about regulating international air space, and nobody has the faintest idea just what this means legally. President Eisenhower has written to Moscow about controlling outer space.

But already the air space of almost every nation is being persistently violated without a hint of protest. Soviet and American satellites, from a purely legal standpoint, are trespassing every moment they are directly above the territory of other than the launching country.

There is not even an approach to accepted definition of national air space. I am indebted to a New York admiralty lawyer, William L. Standard, for pointing out that concepts still employed today remain based on the ancient Roman theory *cujus est solum ejus est usque ad coelum et ad inferos* (he who owns the ground owns everything to the heavens and to the depths).

In 1919 a Paris convention recognized that "every power has complete and exclusive sovereignty over the air space above its territory." This was reasserted by a similar Havana agreement in 1928. The Chicago convention on international civil aviation in 1944 stipulated: "The contracting states recognize that every state has complete and exclusive sovereignty over the air space above its territory."

Our federal air commerce act provides that the United States "is hereby declared to possess and exercise complete and exclusive national sovereignty in the air space above the United States." This, of course, begins immediately above the ground. But how high up does it go?

Various authorities have sought to define some sort of vertical boundary. C. Wilfred Jenks thinks this should be the earth's atmosphere. John Cobb Cooper would place the limit where the world's gravitational power ceases—a nice problem for diplomatists to calculate. Andrew G. Haley would terminate national sovereignty where the regime of aerodynamic lift ends and the regime of Kepler force takes over. Haley, a Washington lawyer, thinks the upper border should be fifty miles, but Sir Leslie Munro, former president of the U.N. Assembly, already speculates about sovereignty over celestial bodies eventually reached by man. Until old Roman law is modified by international accord, anybody's sputnik violates everybody's air space.

There are various tricky aspects. Satellites launched so far have been strictly peaceful. But were a satellite carrying a bomb to be triggered off in war, it would have to be detached over Scandinavia or China to hit America—because of the orbiting sputnik's speed. This might involve neutral nations.

And who owns what comes down? The Russians claimed a rocket fragment from Sputnik I that fell in Alaska. Is it theirs? And how about pollution of the upper atmosphere? Thermonuclear test explosions certainly intrude on other powers' air space by scattering radioactive elements. Can other nations bring suit before The Hague International Court of Justice?

Each time either we or the Russians touch off a big blast in the Pacific or Siberia, the Japanese complain. Is there any international law on this? In the Trail Smelter case, the United States was indemnified by Canada when sulphur fumes from Trail, British Columbia, polluted the air above the state of Washington. Mr. Standard, from whom much of this information derives, pointed out that in 1907 Georgia was granted an injunction against Tennessee to prevent the discharge and spread of noxious factory gases.

It therefore seems an intriguing anachronism that the nations of the world have not yet even agreed on which of them owns how much of the seven seas, a seemingly simple matter to adjudicate. In the meantime, regulated only by a Roman law which everyone happily ignores, man trespasses the air above him with deadly, high-flying missiles and clouds of scientifically engendered particles of poison. Still higher circulate those intricate mechanical devices projected into space like Pioneer, whose ultimate intentions (knowing man for what he is) are unlikely to remain forever bland.

We must certainly press assiduously to isolate outer space from military exploitation. But a long way remains to go before agreement is achieved on how this abstruse subject can be discussed. So far the Russians express willingness to review it only if the United States simultaneously undertakes to talk over the broad subject of bases on foreign soil. In other words, the U.S.S.R., confident in its current lead in intercontinental missiles, wants to ban American intermediate-range-missile installations before any conference moves into the rarefied upper diplomatic atmosphere.

The Kremlin is not illogical when it wishes to link the subject of space and rockets. The problem will be to bracket missile ramps everywhere—including Cape Canaveral, Novaya

Zemlya, and Siberia—not just those that are extraterritorial. We cannot agree to talk only of IRBMs while leaving the Russians a clear advantage in ICBMs. They are now testing these on an operational basis with nuclear warheads.

Nevertheless, there is direct connection between terrestrial military planning and the unexplored heavens. General Thomas D. White, Chief of Staff of the United States Air Force, observed: "In discussing air and space, it should be recognized that there is no division, *per se,* between the two. For all practical purposes air and space merge, forming a continuous and indivisible field of operations." Future ability to control space will "permit our freedom of movement on the surface of the earth and through the earth's atmosphere."

Statesmen as well as soldiers must study this immensely complicated and incredibly important subject. They must familiarize themselves with definitions that have never before impinged upon diplomacy. There are new terms of measurement: the "astronautical unit"—about 93,000,000 miles; the "light-year"—5.83 trillion miles; and the "parallax second"— 19.15 trillion miles. Man has only begun to penetrate the heavens. Telescopes already can discern distances equivalent to one billion light years. For the sake of convenience, scientists divide the emptiness above us into five categories. The troposphere extends ten miles up. From ten to sixteen miles is the region called the stratosphere. From sixteen to fifty miles is the mesosphere. From there to 300 miles is the range of the thermosphere. And from 300 to 1,000 miles is the exosphere zone.

Men are beginning to investigate each of these bands. The first Soviet sputnik coursed only through the thermosphere and exosphere. But the orbital arcs of the second sputnik, Explorer, and Vanguard have all extended far above the exosphere into true outer space. And Pioneer has penetrated far beyond, toward the moon; its Soviet successor neared the sun.

It is imperative that governments should begin efforts to formulate peaceful means of joining in celestial discoveries before some nation establishes a heavenly position from which it can dominate this planet. Brigadier General Homer A. Boushey, an American expert on aerial research, advocates the moon for strategical uses. The moon's high ground could, General Boushey suggests, serve as a launching point toward Earth for retaliatory missiles with only about 20 per cent of the thrust needed on Earth. These missiles could—thanks to the lack of resistant atmosphere—be launched from shafts sunk into the moon's surface, perhaps even catapulted, with no internal propellant. Once a missile was launched Earthward, the moon-based crew could track and guide it.

Such concepts are fantastic but no longer fanciful. And their potential military implication is immense. Manned platforms in outer space or missile ramps upon the moon would give the controlling nation a seemingly overwhelming advantage from which to dictate. *Air Force* says: "Dr. Edward Teller gave a hint of that prospect during his testimony at a recent Congressional hearing. He was being asked why man would want to go to the moon. And he answered that it would be interesting to find out what was there. Asked later what he thought we might find when we did get there, Dr. Teller answered, 'Russians.' "

It is discouraging to read of these exciting prospects which may so soon enable man to contemplate how minute is his being in this universe and then to realize how apparently intent he is on suicide. One may only hope that if a summit meeting indeed occurs it will begin to systematize exploration of space. Perhaps if this is done, men will eventually recognize that neither national nor ideological differences have quite so weighty a significance as we now believe.

Astonishing speed and scope of scientific developments profoundly affect human relationships. This leads Arthur Koestler to observe: "A process which, once past a critical limit, shows this type of catastrophic acceleration is called in physics an explosion. A dispassionate observer from another world, to whom centuries are as seconds, able to survey the whole curve in one sweep, would have come to the conclusion that our civilization is either on the verge of, or in the process of, exploding. . . ."

The alarming thing is the coincidence of a period of unprecedented spiritual decline with an equally unprecedented increase of power. The Promethean myth seems to be coming true with a horrible twist: the giant reaching out to steal the lightning from the gods is morally insane. Hence the difficulty of persuading mankind even to acquiesce in his own survival.

The task of arranging a pattern for coexistence among frightened and suspicious nations must inevitably be long and tedious. Meetings at the summit can at best but isolate the most urgent problems. Months of negotiating must follow before approximate peace, as distinct from mere absence of holocaust, can be achieved. And then, during years of patient experiment, differing nations and ideologies must learn the habit of dwelling together in tolerance.

The political developments that have occurred during the short lifetime of the United Nations are so prodigious that it is lunacy for that body not to recognize them. No international organization can sensibly hope to influence and restrain the inhibitions and actions of great countries like Communist China without admitting them to its councils. The United Nations cannot regard its constitution as so perfect that, after years of constantly changing conditions, it should not consider modifications.

What is most urgently needed among the powers is to arrange an armistice for the war that has not happened because it is too dangerous to fight. But drafting true peace perhaps cannot even yet be started, for, as President Eisenhower has pointed out, the roots of many problems "are buried deep."

Cold-war armistice is a very special thing. It requires real balance of power stabilized in an atmosphere of some trust. It is more than mere *détente* or absence of open provocation. But it is also a good deal less than peace as the world likes to remember the word's meaning.

The first requisite step is to start some sort of international game of Still Pond, No More Moving. This applies to all nations, big and small, which are trying to extend their influence by artificial means. Mere existence is now too easily capable of sudden extinction.

In 1892 the Swedish inventor of dynamite, Alfred Nobel, observed to a pacifist friend: "My factories may make an end of war sooner than your congresses. The day when two army corps can annihilate each other in one second, all civilized nations, it is to be hoped, will recoil from war and discharge their troops." A few months later he added: "If in thirty years it has not been possible to reform the present system, we shall unavoidably fall back into barbarism."

And yet, during the decades since he first released the power of dynamite, more—and more horrible—wars have ravished the earth. Nobel himself bequeathed his fortune to stimulate peaceful and cultural endeavor. Nevertheless, in 1945, a quantum explosion of energy such as he could never have foreseen eviscerated Hiroshima.

Since that awful instant, man has accelerated the pace at which he solves the mysteries of motion, matter, and their mutations. Prior to fission's discovery, scientists were still groping: poor marksmen, blindfolded, shooting at birds in the darkness of a land where birds were few. All this has astonishingly changed. We are building rockets to launch among the planets. Before long these will be filled with palpitating animals whose terror registers on earth-bound beams. The day is dawning when we can set new worlds spinning, when creatures from this star can flee it into labyrinthine space.

The United States as well as the U.S.S.R. must learn that the two great blocs coexisting are simply not, as Ambrose

Bierce would say, "incompossible." The American cynic created this word to mean: "unable to exist if something else exists; two things are incompossible when the world of being has scope enough for one of them, but not enough for both."

This is a condition of thinking that we must eliminate from our own thoughts as a nation and from the foreign policy that expresses these thoughts. In this respect, I would like to quote a few words from a speech Kennan gave in Pittsburgh in 1956: "We Americans, in particular, must learn to act more normally toward Russian people, to remember that they are human beings like ourselves, to get over the charged and excited quality we have contrived to insert into every relationship with them. . . . If American foreign policy were to be addressed exclusively to righting the wrongs of the past rather than to developing the possibilities of the present, it would have a long way to go. . . ."

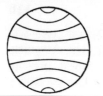

Chapter 5

Flaws in Our Only Grand Alliance

The most important commitment of our foreign policy is membership in the North Atlantic Treaty Organization. NATO is, without comparison, the weightiest alliance undertaking ever assumed by the United States.

NATO, which was a direct response to the threat of direct Soviet aggression in Western Europe, sprang into existence as a consequence of Stalin's rape of Czechoslovakia. Its conception was helped by the fact that we had already launched the Marshall Plan to rebuild the Continent, and the British and French had created a new military alliance called Western Union.

The idea of a peacetime military coalition, with its international headquarters, commands, logistical arrangements, and standing forces, is without precedent. General Alfred M. Gruenther, who first served as Eisenhower's staff chief and later assumed command of NATO himself, told me once he had been unable to find any similar alliance in history except the first Delian League. This was an organization of Greek city-states some 2,500 years ago.

It is, therefore, of pointed interest to examine the history of the Delian League. It was founded in 478 B.C. at the instigation of Athens, great power of the then Western world. A men-

acing Persian expedition from the East had been repulsed
and Greek civilization saved from destruction. The Athenian
statesman Aristides resolved to organize a coalition to prevent
any new threat. The league was conceived as a free confederation of autonomous cities and was founded with the object
of protecting its members against common danger from Asia.
It was led by Athens because that state had the predominant
war-making power. Although the league was inspired and led
by the superstate Athens, its capital was at Delos. Alliance
leaders met there in synod, a rather rudimentary NATO
Council.

During the first decade, the league carried on a cold war
against the Persians and reduced their remaining European
strongholds. However, as fears of another invasion subsided,
the league's vitality ebbed. Athens, nevertheless, remained
aware of the possibility of a recurrent menace. It began to interfere with the local autonomy of lagging smaller allies. Under
agreements with them, it established garrisons on their territory. But Athens' allies resented her demands that her soldiers, in the event of altercations with citizens of other states,
be tried only by Athenian courts.

A. R. Burn in his excellent book *Pericles and Athens*
writes: "The trouble was that the keen, efficient Athenians,
who had become inured to business-like habits during the
training of the new navy and the great war itself, found the
Ionians and islanders chronically slow and unmilitary.

"To the island farmers, fishermen and small traders, it
seemed to matter very little if a contingent (for the league's
common defense forces) was a ship or two short of its quota
or arrived a little late at its rendez-vous. The allies resented
these exactions and this insistence on punctuality (demanded
by the Athens-dominated synod), and found the Athenians'
undisguised consciousness of superior efficiency none the
more welcome from the fact that it was justified.

"Moreover, as the years passed and the apparent Persian

danger receded, compulsory naval service became increasingly unpopular. . . . The intermittent friction which is, alas, almost a normal feature of relations between allies, became exacerbated until throughout the Aegean the Athenians, though still admired, were generally unpopular. The enthusiasm of the early days waned rapidly."

The Delian League existed in theory until 404 B.C. Nevertheless, after the first few vigorous years in the face of obvious menace, its force began perceptibly to wane. It finally dissolved when Athens, the citadel of democracy, was captured by an autocratic Sparta possessed of a mighty land army.

Is there not a ghastly lesson in this memory? In terms of relative power, America is the Athens of NATO; Paris is its Delos. Our insistence upon defensive contributions by smaller allies meets with increasing unpopularity. Terms of compulsory service are criticized, although we have avoided one Athenian mistake by allowing our soldiers on foreign bases to be tried for civil offenses in local courts.

But our continual insistence that the present Eastern danger remains real, if not apparent, is resented by those who wish to take Moscow's post-Stalin approach at better than face value. Our "consciousness of superior efficiency" in military matters is "not welcome although justified." And several allies tend more and more to be a "ship or two short" or to "arrive a little late."

The circumstances of fear that inspired NATO's creation —just like those of the Delian League—have altered. Our alliance is discernibly slipping. The founding ardor has faded. We must seek new methods to invigorate the psychological will to common effort without which the coalition is doomed. One may take comfort in the fact that the Delian League did last several decades despite its tragic decline. But what was the final end? The destruction of democracy.

The change in Soviet tactics during recent years and the strategic revolution that forces ever-heavier reliance upon nuclear weapons have combined to weaken NATO's early vigor. This is not the fault of the generals who command the alliance's military forces. They do their best to plan emergency defense in constantly changing circumstances. But they cannot possibly succeed unless their governments support them more. The trend is down, not up.

The commanders themselves admit the coalition has little validity unless it can protect the bulk of its territory and population from initial conquest in case of war. Today such hopes are still a dream. In 1952, NATO talked of building up to ninety-six divisions. Even on paper, less than a third of these exist. Aircraft and missiles cannot alone fill the gap.

It was reckoned that two continental powers would share the main manpower burden—France and West Germany. Yet today France's contribution is virtually worthless. All her NATO divisions have been stripped of infantry to quell the Algerian uprising. Remaining artillery, ordnance companies, headquarters staffs, and signal corps cannot face sudden aggression. The Bonn republic is now at last on the road to furnishing twelve atomic-age divisions. German negotiators once spoke of augmenting this pledge to nineteen. But their army was delayed for many months in parliamentary corridors. Now there is talk in almost every NATO land of paring down levels even further. The United States and England rely increasingly upon their own strategic air and missile power. In such a mood, their NATO ground garrisons are steadily being reduced.

The moment British and American troops begin to trickle out of Germany, what is left of Europe's determination to defend itself may vanish. That would force a drastic change in plans. Supreme Headquarters, Allied Powers in Europe might have to reckon, in the event of war, on abandoning most of the Continent, banking on final victory through air power and another painful liberation. Such strategic decisions would magnify the political danger. One country after the other could be tempted to make accommodations with Moscow, seeking neutrality pacts like those Hitler held forth to little nations before he devoured them.

The Kremlin has succeeded brilliantly in creating a new climate. Latent divergencies within the free democracies have been encouraged. Their will to build defensive strength is ebbing. And, by inducing the West to reduce military budgets, the Russian leaders hope to eliminate what they see as a prop sustaining the capitalist economies. Does the U.S.S.R. think it is offering us a few years of ease at the end of which lies depression or defeat?

NATO has not responded adequately to the altered threat. Our statesmen offer the populations of the West the platitudes of linguistic ritual. They speak the truth softly and the falsehood loudly. They tell us we have never been so strong, safe, or determined. But one does not defeat a messianic system such as Soviet imperialism with wishful thinking. Nor does one devise an adequate police force by whittling it away.

The permanent political organization of NATO was handicapped from the start. Member governments show little spirit of team play when it comes to their individual problems. There, because it has no real power, the alliance Council is forced to pussyfoot. When needed, it was never realistically able to discuss Trieste. It dodged Cyprus until that crisis exploded all over the Mediterranean and opened an avenue to Soviet Middle Eastern penetration. In French North Africa, it has managed to exert scant influence.

These are disturbing facts. If they are not faced squarely, it may be too late for salvage. History has shown that any alliance is bound ultimately to dwindle: its validity and success can only be tested by ability to survive the critical periods that inspired its necessity.

Surely our own critical period has not yet passed. We cannot reckon that a Soviet dictatorship, still heavily armed, still worshiping Lenin's doctrine of ultimate world triumph, is suddenly a great big Switzerland. When NATO was born, Western civilization was menaced. It remains menaced, politically, economically, militarily, and it must be willing to defend itself.

Lord Ismay, NATO's former secretary general, used to tell of the villagers who built a wall along their dangerous mountain road. For some years afterward, no swerving automobiles plunged into the abyss below. Then the barrier began to crumble. But the villagers refused to pay for its repair. "Why should we?" they inquired of each other. "Let's save money. There have been no accidents for so long a time."

The cause for NATO's decline is refusal by its members to delegate to the alliance even a modicum of authority over their individual national affairs. In this attitude the great powers—Britain, France, and the United States—have taken the lead. Their smaller colleagues, right down to tiny Iceland, have followed suit.

Various reasons for failure to co-operate are adduced. The British, for example, argue they cannot associate more closely with Europe in supranational accords because of their Commonwealth interests. But Canada's Foreign Secretary told the alliance Council that Commonwealth countries *want* Britain to co-operate more actively with Europe.

The French, with the supersensitivity of a declining empire, demand a greater authority but resent allied advice in the explosive North African situation. They argue that North Africa is their affair. Nevertheless, NATO's military command specifically includes the entire area from eastern Tunisia to western Morocco (in a secret 1952 directive).

And how about the United States? As undisputed leader of the coalition, we have been free with counsel to all our friends. We opposed our two major allies, Britain and France, over Suez. We insisted that France should take a "liberal" attitude in Africa. We demanded a European Defense Community even after such a project was no longer feasible.

In what ways do we now endeavor to assert our leadership? We cannot, as we explain, subject American national authority to international controls or further extend our pledges of co-operation. Our Constitution forbids this. Our Congress would not tolerate it. Nevertheless, if we want allies—and we need them almost as much as they need us—we will have to take some initiative to restore their slowly sagging confidence even if this requires special sacrifices or legislative changes, for example, giving our friends access to some of our nuclear weapons.

Apologies about our constitutional restrictions are not enough. There are ways of asserting imaginative leadership. In 1951 and 1952 no one doubted the political vigor and diplomatic audacity of the United States. We sent to NATO our most brilliant officers, including Eisenhower, Gruenther, and Lauris Norstad. We appointed a special embassy which included three ambassadors—headed by Averell Harriman, a man of great ability and European reputation. But by 1956 Secretary Dulles confided to diplomatic colleagues that one trouble with NATO was that ambassadors to its permanent Council were of insufficient international stature and inadequately briefed by their governments. If this is so, whose fault is it? If our own envoys are not considered sufficiently prominent, who named them? And if they are not completely briefed, does not the State Department brief them?

This is no effort to be captious. The truth is that Dulles put his finger on a weak spot. We can recapture leadership and stir allied imagination if we take some bold new step. The United States could galvanize new interest in the alliance by sending a man of outstanding renown as it envoy. What would be wrong with emphasizing America's bipartisan concern with NATO and determination to build it up by appointing the defeated presidential nominee for at least one year as our ambassador to the alliance Council? Statesmen in both our parties insist NATO is the foundation of our foreign policy.

Therefore, it should be our most important diplomatic mission.

Were such a superenvoy named, he would attract vast attention among Europeans now being led into irresolute doldrums by clever Soviet propaganda. He would be in a position to make weighty policy recommendations which, because of their sponsor's importance, might particularly influence Congress. This is the kind of bipartisan leadership our allies desire from us. The job could add little luster to the name of so distinguished an American. Acceptance would represent immense personal sacrifice. It would be sheer public service. But it might transform the alliance. For NATO to be resuscitated, it must be dramatized.

Were we to make this striking gesture, there is no telling what our friends might be induced to do. There are outstanding statesmen available and retired in other coalition countries. Can we not take a lead in transforming the alliance Council into what it really ought to be—the most important democratic agency to oversee protection of our civilization?

While strongly denying it, both the United States and Britain appear to be altering their conceptions of NATO's usefulness and modifying their military strategy. Each is clearly preparing to place much heavier reliance upon its own long-range nuclear air power and less upon the idea of defending Western Europe on the ground.

Economically, more protection is provided at less cost if we rely upon atomic weapons. But politically, this concept leads to dangerous possibilities. In logic, it infers that any incident considered provocative enough to warrant war must henceforth risk hydrogen war. Furthermore, if our allies see reduction in Anglo-American troop commitments on the Continent, they will almost certainly abate their own defensive efforts. The probable consequence of this would be neutralism and arguments for individual nonaggression pacts with Moscow.

If allied strategy is based primarily upon nuclear ripostes

to aggression, are we not doomed to inaction in the event of any Soviet move that is not clearly an all-out attack? What, for example, would we do if Russia occupied some non-NATO country like Finland or Yugoslavia? What action did we take when the U.S.S.R. raped Hungary? Did we deem such provocation worth courting world destruction?

Surely if we reduce our overseas forces, the European allies will show less interest in self-protection. They would reason there is nothing they can do to change the balance of atomic war; they might be destroyed, occupied, and eventually liberated, but, feeling powerless to act significantly, they would slip into lassitude.

One effect of this could be an increasing desire to terminate base arrangements that help make Anglo-American air power more effective. This would handicap the very type of strategy Washington and London are developing. Therefore, too much emphasis on air power might ultimately make us weaker while simultaneously putting a bonus on limited aggression.

NATO's military commanders are trying to solve this puzzle. They are developing plans for European defense with a minimum of manpower but without relying on weapons more terrible than tactical atomic projectiles. If sufficient new arms devised by American scientists can be distributed along various North Atlantic sectors, this strategy is feasible. Unfortunately, such devices are not reaching the Continent in anything like the requisite volume.

Under prevailing circumstances, the alliance must reconcile itself to continuation of either an American commander in chief or an American chief of staff. This is necessary because of our law limiting the sharing of atomic secrets—on which European defense depends. This United States ascendancy poses particular psychological problems. To help us understand them, it might be useful for small detachments of European troops to be stationed as garrisons in the United States.

It might aid both sides of the Atlantic to comprehend problems caused by foreign military dispositions and command.

Apart from long-range strategic considerations arising as NATO enters a new phase, serious political and economic problems are now being studied. The West must agree on an effective military force to police its borders for a period of indefinite duration. And it must also decide how to meet the economic challenge of the Soviet bloc. Communism seeking to expand throughout the world can compete and infiltrate by ordering its subjects to pull in their belts. This challenge must be faced.

It is paradoxically possible that Communism may sacrifice some of its magnetic appeal as it begins to normalize its methods. If, during coming years, de-Stalinization makes of the Bolshevik party something beginning to approach other political organizations, it is likely to lose fanatical fervor. Yet it was this fervor that in the past mesmerized feckless, discontented people around the world. Many human beings, like moths, are attracted by dangerous bright flames. The very single-mindedness of purpose, the blatant narrowness of Communism helped to conquer minds that could digest only the simplest of ideas. Weak men often require a crutch. This is sometimes the appeal of authoritarian systems.

Of course, even under most favorable circumstances it will be long before Communism relinquishes both its dictatorial straitness and its passion. But should it do so, it might someday begin to resemble other more mature and less dynamic parties. And if that time ever arrives, this very relaxation is sure to be mirrored abroad by diminished ardor among bolshevism's admirers. Such conjecture, however, remains both theoretical and distant. Meanwhile, we in the West must remain on our guard, for Communist Russia is still a monolithic, autocratic state. There are no protective checks and balances within its system, no free press or parliamentary debate to insure against eventual return to methods of brutal menace.

The democracies must avoid any dangerous relaxation as Communism experiments with the agonies of change. We must hold to our course, determined never to start a war but to deter others from doing so. NATO is the main expression of this policy. That alliance is experiencing difficulty as a result of the easing of apparent danger. Yet it must survive. If the West can stay united during the period of strains that is bound eventually to ensue within the Soviet bloc, it may eventually attain its principal objectives.

If ever Communism allows a "liberal" spirit to develop, Moscow will be constrained to loosen its grip upon the satellites. Then, even if they retain socialistic forms, they are bound to resume many natural ties with the West. At such a time, the U.S.S.R. would find it more difficult to prevent free unification of Germany.

Meanwhile, NATO must not dissolve. Autocratic Russia can always reassemble its dutiful satellite alliance and reassert authority, whereas to build a voluntary democratic coalition is both tedious and difficult.

We in the West should take comfort from the fact that Moscow now professes more peaceful intent. The Kremlin has decided to release several hundred thousand soldiers. But we must remember that military planners on both sides of the ideological curtain are reconciling themselves to the technological revolution. During World War II their concept was to use troops supported by weapons. The Russians themselves, who had enormous reservoirs of manpower, protected precious tanks and heavy guns with screens of human flesh. Now, in the age of tactical atomic arms, planning everywhere has been revised. Weapons are supported by troops, not vice versa.

The West had already adjusted to this idea. It realized that far fewer soldiers, behind an atomic screen, can hold great segments of the Continent if anyone is mad enough to start a war. Moscow, too, is clearly aware of this. The Russians are releasing redundant manpower, no longer militarily essential, for use in factory and field.

Can our alliance ever be made viable in any but a military sense? Will the allies ever agree to support one another's views outside the treaty area, as France wishes and we do not? Could they even cease to contradict one another in international forums?

This last is vitally important. An analysis of U.N. voting records produces something of a shock. During ten debates in 1957, fourteen NATO members (West Germany is not yet in the United Nations) expressed themselves on everything from African economic aid to means of defining aggression. In only one of these discussions did the North Atlantic powers cast a unanimous ballot. This was for a resolution urging continued efforts to realize U.N. objectives in Korea. On everything else there was disagreement in varying degree. For example, Greece, which had been hysterically shopping about for Afro-Asian support on its Cyprus claims, opposed the rest of NATO on five unrelated matters. Either by contrary vote or by abstention, Belgium, Portugal, and Denmark marched alone on other points. France did not participate in the balloting on Algeria. There was a wide-open split in the NATO attitude toward racism in South Africa.

It is, of course, impossible to arrange a binding compact committing the partners to an all-for-one and one-for-all opinion on every subject. But it is deeply distressing to find how often we and our allies work against one another and therefore against the common interest. Is it not possible to devise some dignified formula to preserve at least appearances of unity? Should not a minimal obligation of alliance be that members will at least abstain from voting on disputed topics rather than trying to knock one another down? Every time one ally opposes another a residue of permanent friction remains.

We ourselves seemed for a long time to feel, for example, that if we backed France on Algeria or the Netherlands on

West New Guinea, we might prejudice our position in newly independent lands. But could we not make our point sufficiently merely by always abstaining rather than negating? Surely the nations of the free world would recognize the meaning of such abstention were NATO's membership formally to adopt an obligation not to vote against its own majority except, perhaps, on subjects such as Cyprus; in other words, on matters solely concerning NATO members. And on such matters, would it not be far more dignified for the allies to promise to settle them among themselves rather than placing them upon the public podium?

Any alliance contains inherent disruptive forces. If these are not curbed, the coalition is doomed to eventual disintegration. Yet nobody has come up with any pat formula to handle NATO's obvious centrifugal trends. Even if no answer is entirely satisfactory, would it not be wise to work out some general operating method?

Were each North Atlantic ally to pledge itself never to oppose the majority on public votes but, if deemed necessary, merely to register disapproval by abstention, some of the more passionate discords shattering the alliance would at least be allowed to cool. This should be made an obligation of membership in the pact. The subject, unfortunately, has never been squarely faced. But it would certainly not be overwhelmingly difficult to achieve a satisfactory *modus operandi* acceptable to all North Atlantic governments.

To date, our own view that NATO commitments apply only to the specified area of the pact has been argued with religious fervor. So has the European view that these commitments apply the world around. But this is not a question of theology. This is a question of diplomacy, whose very essence is compromise. Obviously, if an alliance is to have any real meaning it must learn to compromise within itself.

During the past few years there has been a perceptible easing in allied resolve. This is noticeable in the United States, leader of the coalition. Long before the modest North Atlantic military goals had been achieved, we began unilaterally to cut our forces. When Moscow started an extensive program of Asian economic aid, we minimized this as a "one-shot" effort. We juggled comparative figures to show how gigantic our industrial production was without allowing for gadgets and chromium bumpers.

This approach induced happy unconcern, and the mood was, of course, contagious. Britain and France pared defenses. West Germany reduced the scale of its pledged rearmament. Centrifugal tendencies began to rend the coalition. Only the launching of Sputnik I jarred us back to reality. But too many leaders and too many bureaucrats still confuse post-sputnik Russia with pre-sputnik Russia. They talk of Khrushchev's troubles with the satellites, economic difficulties, and popular apathy. This is all true, but it is merely part of the picture. The emphasis is crazily wrong.

When Harry Hopkins first met Stalin in 1941, he reported that the dictator "thought one weakness the British had was underrating their enemy; he did not propose to do this." Are we again tending in the same direction?

Post-sputnik Russia is making every effort to awe the world with its strength. Its foreign policy will inevitably become more relentless. The aims of this policy are evident: preserving unity within the Communist bloc; freezing the *status quo* in Europe, including a partitioned Germany; exploiting Afro-Asian nationalism; splitting NATO and shoving the United States from foreign bases. This was Kremlin strategy before the development of long-range missiles. And even at that time Moscow showed truculence. Now it is rapidly establishing a new position of strength. Is it not therefore logical to anticipate bolder efforts at intimidation? For this we must be both forewarned and forearmed.

No matter how shabby Russian living standards may appear to statistics-ridden Westerners, the base of Soviet power is threateningly strong. This is what NATO fails to emphasize—even to itself. The U.S.S.R.'s aid offensive in the Middle East costs less than one tenth of 1 per cent of its national income. In return, trade with that area has almost tripled in three years. And Moscow has established a mortgage on Syria and Egypt, now federated, by selling them overvalued, often obsolescent arms. Time alone will prove whether Nasser can escape this economic grip.

The Soviets are currently short on labor because of low wartime birth rates. Despite this, compulsory school attendance has been extended until the age of seventeen in order to press for world technical ascendancy, although students are now liable to a temporary labor draft. And Khrushchev, whose record of achievement is impressive, boasts Russia will attain United States meat, milk, and butter consumption levels by 1962, end its housing shortage by 1970, and equal American production by 1972.

While still needing to import engineering machinery, Moscow exports capital goods to uncommitted nations—for political prestige. And the Kremlin has emerged as neutralism's and nationalism's proclaimed champion. It has registered huge gains in Syria, Egypt, Iraq, Afghanistan, and Indonesia. Up to one thousand of its trusted technicians are scattered throughout the Middle East. And, in addition to all this, the U.S.S.R. maintains an incredibly strong military establishment.

All these gloomy facts were true before Sputnik I was launched. And it is apparent that the situation may get worse before it stands a chance of getting better. Such being the case, why is there no greater atmosphere of urgency? Western statesmen again begin to talk the way they did when they were drafting plans for paper armies they comfortably forgot. Again one hears assurances that there really is no need to hurry. Cannot the West hear hurrying footsteps at its back?

At the end of 1957, to face this problem jointly, NATO's chiefs of government held their one and only summit meeting.

The sole philosophical document, if such it can be called, that issued from this was a Paris "declaration" endorsed by the fifteen allied powers. It was by intention a kind of democratic manifesto, a statement of principles. It was designed to stress to the entire world NATO's resolution to defend a certain way of life, but, at the same time, its earnest hopes to preserve peace and adhere to the rules of the United Nations.

The history of this proclamation is worth examining. On November 27, 1957, after the permanent North Atlantic Council had decided some such public exposition was desirable, an initial draft was composed in the name of Secretary General Paul-Henri Spaak. This was then circulated to various capitals and subjected to the editing processes of allied foreign ministries. These processes were drastic. When the final version, approved by the heads of government, emerged, it was more than twice as long, somewhat more elegantly couched, less direct, and certainly more ideological than Spaak's original. There is no doubt that the fifteen-nation definitive copy was on the whole better written. But there is doubt that the finer language produced a more magnetic appeal.

The vital question revolves around the word "communism." Spaak is an eminently sensible man, a Socialist of the most vigorously democratic variety who has actually made a serious study of Marxism. He does not have a fixation on the phrase "international communism," which creeps into so many speeches and articles, for example, by our own fluent Secretary of State. Therefore, in his first draft, Spaak did not single out Moscow's ideology. Instead, sensibly, he merely reaffirmed the coalition's intention of opposing "any aggression whatsoever."

The fifteen nations were not content to let well enough alone. They insisted on interjecting two rather unnecessary phrases which have little to do with self-defense as such but everything to do with state philosophy. In paragraph six of the declaration as ultimately accepted, this sentence was in-serted: "The free world faces the mounting challenge of inter-national communism backed by Soviet power." In paragraph seven, the approved draft spoke of the "peoples under inter-national Communist rule" being "sacrificed to the purposes of world domination and military power."

This, naturally, suited Dulles, who is a devoutly religious man and detests Communism because it is avowedly atheistic. But that is no reason to try to turn NATO into a second anti-Comintern pact. Its purpose is not to squash another ide-ology, but to defend its members against aggression. This applies to any kind of aggression. Let us suppose, for exam-ple, that a convulsion in Russia suddenly produced a military dictatorship that disavowed Communism but reavowed im-perialist intentions. Such could prove just as menacing to NATO as the present system.

Our enemy is not Communism per se, but Soviet imperial-ism and the threat of attack from any hostile quarter regard-less of its present or future ideology. Our purpose is to pro-tect ourselves and our allies. That is all.

Such being the case, why do we persist in confusing our-selves? Denouncing Marxism is popular in the United States. But if the Paris declaration hoped to attract support in other areas of the world, it would be better to forget ideological pretensions and stick to self-defense, life, liberty, and the pursuit of happiness.

Our own present administration has obstinately confused itself on this despite efforts to court Yugoslavia and Poland. In 1952 General Eisenhower prepared his only report as NATO commander. In the first version of this document he had referred numerous times to "international communism." Eisenhower was kind enough to consult me on this and I ar-gued that it would be wiser to substitute for that phrase other more realistic expressions such as "Soviet imperialism," or "Russian expansionism." This was done. But, after more editing, the ultimate draft emerged with all references to "international communism" back.

This is plain silly. Why mix our political and military aims with our ideological preferences? United States policy is not to develop an anti-Comintern pact any more than it was once to develop an antifascist league. And NATO's *raison d'être* is not as a holy alliance.

Both our own and North Atlantic Treaty policies are geared to the United Nations. Nowhere in that body's legal structure is there expressed preferment for one or another system. Peace, opposition to aggression, and the right to self-defense remain the common link.

One reason for NATO's confusion is that, in a fashion, the alliance reflects the explosive difficulties erupting within the framework of the hitherto tightly organized Soviet orbit. On each side of the rusting Iron Curtain are arising new forces and unanticipated problems. Both coalitions find themselves faced with changing circumstances, political, military, economic, and psychological. The powers, great and small, are learning that in varying senses we are all becoming "colonies." That is to say, as the world shrinks, it discovers increasing territorial interdependence. Moscow realizes that if freedom is allowed to take roots in Budapest or Warsaw, it must inevitably spread like the tendrils of a banyan tree throughout Russia itself. The U.S.S.R. thus becomes a victim of its own monolithic policy. The further Communism is stretched, the more extended are Moscow's energies in preserving a false philosophy. When Eastern Europe rose up, Soviet troops were forced to perform the same traditional function of colonialism that the Kremlin so often criticizes in others. Thus, in a psychological sense, Russia became a colony of Hungary. It is still subject to the powers of endurance of the incredibly tough Magyar people—or their echoes elsewhere within the imperial realm.

Western consciences were deeply troubled by inability to help the Hungarians without promoting holocaust. This very problem stimulated thought about what should be done if a similar revolt began in East Germany. There is no simple answer. NATO is deeply perplexed. West Germans talk of "armed infiltration" coupled with diplomatic warnings—to give at least some support to any further popular insurrections. But there can never be a guarantee that if partisan movements are supported by NATO members, nuclear war will not be touched off.

The North Atlantic powers find it impossible to agree on how such problems should be faced by military planning. The democracies wish to spend less on mounting defense costs. Each finds that there is only one way to accomplish this aim—by reducing manpower commitments and depending more heavily upon atomic weapons. However, this produces an embarrassing situation. As conventional military dispositions diminish, there is increased reliance upon nuclear rebuttal to aggression. Would a new uprising in Poland or East Germany be worth world suicide? Furthermore, do not the nonatomic powers place themselves totally in the hands of Washington by developing this strategy?

The United States is bound by law not to give nuclear warheads to its allies. It tries to bridge the problem by providing "dual-purpose" weapons. We tell ourselves and our allies that we do not rely solely upon such horrible arms. But, for compelling economic reasons, we keep reducing the size of our forces and agreeing that the other NATO countries may follow suit. The manpower difference is clearly, if reluctantly, to be made up by nuclear firepower.

Russia has now become dependent politically and psychologically upon freezing its empire. If the Soviet bloc explodes more germs of liberty, there is little chance that Communist dictatorship can continue in the U.S.S.R. But we, also, must lean heavily upon other nations. Secretary Dulles tried to balance the contradictory global concerns of the United States and the allied NATO powers while, at the same time, rebuilding solidarity in Europe. Can this, in the end, success-fully be done?

Prior to the NATO summit conference, Dulles conferred with some leading citizens in a search for new ideas. Harold Stassen proposed creation of an international Strategic Air Command. He wanted us to give the North Atlantic commu-nity a special wing of B-47 bombers which would be manned by allied volunteers and controlled by SHAPE. Furthermore, he wished to see NATO as an organization attempt produc-tion of earth satellites. He called for what he described as an outer-space project. On the nonmilitary side, Stassen thought we should again stress our willingness to negotiate with Mos-cow and reaffirm that our objective is world peace. He hoped we could stimulate NATO willingness to co-operate through O.E.E.C. in economic aid to Africa and Asia. He particularly felt that West Germany should contribute heavily to this. Bonn devotes only 4.4 per cent of its gross national product to defense.

Nelson Rockefeller outlined a plan of his own. He asked that the United States make available to our transatlantic allies a nuclear arsenal. With this, he reasoned, Europe could suc-cessfully defend itself against attack without the need for com-mitting ourselves to an all-out war with Russia.

He also endorsed a joint system of U.S.-NATO weapons research and technical co-operation. He asked for a similar commission to explore peacetime uses of atomic energy. Rockefeller, like Stassen, thought NATO should develop its own variety of Colombo Plan to help underdeveloped countries. Paul Nitze, once head of the State Department's Policy Planning Staff, recommended we give nuclear arms to our allies, keeping them in American custody during peacetime and under SHAPE control during war.

Undoubtedly, certain of these ideas are useful. And most people Dulles consulted agreed that we have hampered both ourselves and our allies hitherto by erecting artificial curtains around some of our military devices and by overly restricting exchanges of information between scientists on both sides of the Atlantic. Recognition of this at least is a big step forward.

One reason for a persistent and bothersome anemia in NATO is the alliance's lack of essential political machinery. There cannot be full harmony among the governmental systems of such diverse countries as the United States, Great Britain, Portugal, and Turkey. But there can and must be full and mutual consultation. A glaring alliance weakness has been the refusal—in order to avoid embarrassment—to face its own internal problems. This lack of frankness fostered a lack of mutual trust.

The United States always considered its North Atlantic political commitments as referring only to a carefully prescribed treaty area. We were prepared to defend our European allies in Europe—but, if desirable, to disregard their trans-maritime interests. This kind of arrangement was tidy for us and convenient for our imperial allies. But it does not make adequate sense. The biggest political problems straining the NATO structure involve what we call colonies.

The Cyprus dispute among Britons, Greeks, and Turks was permitted to disrupt the coalition's eastern flank. The Algerian revolution caused France to remove virtually all infantry effectives from Europe. Yet for years, both problems were almost totally ignored in NATO's Council.

A diplomatic conspiracy, masked in decorous formulas, was permitted to develop. It was decided with Venetian courtesy that matters crucial to the alliance's very heart would be bypassed. The fifteen allies buried their heads politely in the sand. It was, therefore, not illogical that a Suez crisis could develop from this ostrich system. A few French politicians prevailed upon a few British politicians to settle by violence disputes extraterritorial to the alliance.

Despite its internal torments, it is evident that the reasons for the North Atlantic Treaty are quite as valid today as when

Stalin was alive. The danger to liberty is as visible as ever. And all over the free world there are new reasons to huddle together in fear. Surely such a moment must be seized by the ministers of the West to alter the philosophical bonds and tenets of their compact.

Henceforth, it is plain, no coalition can have validity unless all problems involving its material future are threshed out in its councils. Without such co-operation, there can be no valid future for the great Western entente. Areas quite outside NATO's rigid geographical boundaries are involved increasingly in the alliance's political heart.

The Baghdad Pact—which we invented but did not join— is at death's door. But the implications to all of NATO's membership must be considered. What will be done with SEATO, an obligation to which the three greatest NATO members are committed? Should this be brushed under the same rug that for so long hid Cyprus and Algeria? And colonialism? Can the United States afford forever to assume a holy, Jeffersonian attitude while at the same time maintaining *de facto* controls in areas like Okinawa?

These questions must be faced more frankly and more fearlessly than in the past. Otherwise, the North Atlantic alliance is doomed eventually to disintegrate. The moment is not too late. However, this chance must be seized. The situation in Europe changes swiftly. Now is the time to reform, refurbish, and revivify the alliance—above all, its consultative machinery. It cannot any longer remain a military reality beneath an empty political façade.

As yet there is no agreement among the partners on whether they should support each other's global interests or limit mutual obligations to the area defined in the treaty. There are two wholly uncompromising views. France reasons: If the Atlantic Pact has a local character, limited to a precise frontier, and if outside that frontier the interests of allied powers are found to be in opposition or are ignored, it would be particularly grave, above all, for France and Britain. What meaning would the pact have, and how could one escape fears that public opinion and then the governments would not come to doubt the value of an alliance so limited? How could one not fear that all of Europe might slide toward that idea of neutrality which would separate so profoundly the free world and weaken especially the United States?

De Gaulle crystallized these thoughts in his request for the formation of a United States-British-French political directorate of allied world-wide strategy. But this idea is bitterly opposed by NATO's membership. Dulles himself believes we cannot commit ourselves to supporting NATO outside Europe. He claims this would force us into collision with non-European allies or with neutral countries we seek to attract. But he admits differences between what he calls the "alliance approach" and the "collective-defense approach." He says European members of NATO believe allies should back each other's political positions everywhere. He opposes this. He thinks it would force the United States to appear as a sponsor of colonialism. Furthermore, Dulles thinks it unrealistic to talk of strengthening North Atlantic ties by federation. No nation would consider surrendering a portion of its sovereignty during peacetime.

The Secretary of State moralistically wants to treat all our allies as equals. But is it not foolish to contemplate the simplified idea that we have no second-class allies? On the contrary, there is an entire hierarchy. We cannot consider Britain's MacMillan and the Dominican Republic's Trujillo as equal in importance. We do not have to do precisely the same thing in the same degree for each of our partners everywhere. We would become inflexible, stranded between inadequacy and unrealism.

We must face up to the fact that we do indeed have first-, second- and third-class allies. Otherwise, we risk reducing all alliances, including NATO, to the lowest common denominator.

It is important that we should not blind ourselves by loose and simplified thinking. Certainly we must support our NATO partners wherever possible or eventually we will not have a NATO. And that is what Moscow hopes. We can never hazard abandoning our only viable alliance, that in Europe, for indecisive compacts elsewhere. Such is the road to isolation.

Yet, while we preach the need for consultation, we have been loath to practice it. We do not bind ourselves to the decisions of others merely by consulting—as we beg them to do with us. Of course, no nation can be expected to commit itself a priori to the views of its friends. That would mean abdication of sovereignty. But all should practice the obligation to confer or the coalition will sicken. In NATO, as in other spheres of life, one cannot have one's cake and eat it.

We are deeply bothered and unnecessarily embarrassed by the fact that NATO links us to imperial powers. This exaggerated anxiety of ours is, if anything, further complicated by the fact that empires are dissolving. And the dissolution of great empires, even when gradual, has always been a painful process. This was true of Rome, Spain, and Ottoman Turkey. It is true again today of Britain and of France. Although both London and Paris continue to rule over agglomerations of foreign peoples and to influence former dominions, no one can argue that either capital any longer represents the superstate it was so recently. This produces a certain psychological sensitivity which we must comprehend.

Most of Queen Victoria's immense legacy has been lost, including the subcontinent of India and all but peripheral vestiges of the Middle East. Britain is being urged slowly out of Africa and Asia, although the process may take years to complete. Even tiny Jordan, a geographical fiction, was able in 1956 to twist the aging lion's tail.

France is no longer even the second power of continental Europe. With astonishing swiftness, it has been forced to relinquish the Levant states, Indochina, and the last dots of India. Reluctantly it has been driven from Morocco and Tunisia. Now nationalism simmers in sub-Saharan Africa.

Almost necessarily, the elements of the present world situation force the United States to try to ride two policy horses simultaneously. We admire and respect Britain and France, our most important allies. We wish to strengthen their position and assuage their national pride. Yet, at the same time, from the moment of our political birth we have implicitly and explicitly opposed the theory of colonialism.

In this attitude there is paradox. Many Americans are unaware of the essential contradiction between our pious, categorical anticolonial sentiments and the parallel maintenance of authority in distant Panama, Guam, and Okinawa. But the British and French, rendered increasingly touchy as their own possessions dwindle, do not relish this inconsistency.

No empire willingly dissolves itself. But to maintain imperial authority, a nation requires both physical force and moral will. As De Gaulle observed once to me: "France cannot retain its overseas position unless it first restores its own *élan vital.*" This, despite De Gaulle's own efforts, has not yet been achieved. However, the general is clearly seeking to alter the entire structure of the former French empire by his new approach to a commonwealth solution.

Britain, despite extensive pump-priming from the United States (a four-billion-dollar loan and a great chunk of Marshall Plan aid), has not yet fully managed to readjust its economy and can never restore its world position. No longer does it have the resources to act with total international freedom. Yet London continues to pretend to such a role. The habits of power and prestige are difficult to shed.

It is this sad but inevitable situation that brings such poignancy to the Algerian and Cyprus debates. Had France and

Britain remained true great powers there would have been no such discussion. Nationalistic discontent would simply never have been permitted to fester. There is, for example, no U.N. argument scheduled on Latvia or Uzbekistan, for, within the Soviet empire, might continues to make right—as so brutally it did in Hungary.

As the remaining fragments of these empires slip away to independence, we, with our alliance bonds and simultaneous anticolonialist pretensions, are hooked by the cruel dilemma's other horn, for we somewhat arrogantly consider that it is our express dispensation to bear the ark of the liberties of the world. Wilson formulated this feeling in political terms. Roosevelt echoed it. Eisenhower remains bound to its uncomfortable, if high-minded, tenet. How do we plan to apply it in the great double test now facing our allies and their dissatisfied subject peoples?

Because of such fundamental problems, NATO has been forced to remain almost purely a military alliance—which it was not meant to be—with great ideological differences among its members and greater ones among associate bodies. A comparison of the governing methods of Portugal, Turkey, Denmark, and France would be provocative. And they, as a group, are associated through the Balkan Pact with assertively Communist Yugoslavia and through the United States with reactionary Spain.

Article 2 of the Atlantic Treaty, providing for "economic collaboration," has been largely ignored. The stiffening of military defense has had total priority. Furthermore, the Organization for European Economic Cooperation, which includes neutral states, is already in the economic field. NATO has a different membership. Neither Sweden nor Switzerland conceive their duties to O.E.E.C. as involving NATO obligations.

NATO has never grown into the kind of global rallying center for defense that many of its founders dreamed of. There are several other coalitions created for the purpose of regional defense; the moribund Balkan Entente, including Yugoslavia; SEATO, linking three NATO powers to Southeast Asia; the ailing Northern Tier in the Middle East; ANZUS, the alliance of Australia, New Zealand, and the U.S.; and the American alliance with Japan. The result of this messy tangle of commitments, all of which involve NATO members in obligations that might lead to general war, is confusion and division.

Genial, shrewd Lord Ismay wrote as long ago as August 1951: "Even if every quarter of the globe is covered by these regional pacts, there will still be a grave hiatus at the summit. Foreign policy and strategy are indivisible. They cannot be conducted in separate areas with artificial geographical boundaries. . . . What is required, and most urgently required, is some sort of supreme council with world-wide conspectus and world-wide authority. . . ."

There is no doubt that the rather sloppy arrangement now prevailing in free world commitments has to be tidied up even if it is impossible for Denmark to commit itself on its reaction should Cambodia go Communist and even if Switzerland cannot permit its membership in O.E.E.C. to lead to military links with NATO. The smaller NATO powers themselves already dislike the Big Three military "standing group" in Washington and would probably quit the alliance rather than see its political equivalent formed. Yet the existing system is inadequate.

In a speech, Bernard Baruch asked the question: "Have we devised a global strategy to replace the disjointed and piece-meal responses with which, for so long, we met the Soviet challenge?" The answer to that is no. So far we are only moving slowly in the right direction. As Ismay used to say: "We are groping our way toward the light." But groping is not good enough.

The only solution—and a perfectly feasible one if NATO

has any resilience—is for that organization to create a political hierarchy similar to its military and economic structure. The fifteen members must recognize the need to thrash out diplomatic matters among themselves in the precise fashion they discuss intricate if strictly martial matters.

NATO was not originally conceived as a policy-making board. Its genesis was that of any alliance—common interest in self-preservation. But already it has found that, in this complex world, more than military considerations are necessary to devise satisfactory defense. For this reason, the coalition agreed to develop a common budget. Having advanced this far, it is surely not illogical to expect diplomatic co-operation. However, this cannot be accomplished merely by asking smaller partners to accept a Big Three political "standing group" similar to the military committee that meets in Washington. West Germany, Italy, and other allies are unwilling to concede their political direction to the United States, Britain, and France, for in each NATO country a civilian government ultimately sits above the military.

What then? Spaak, Ismay's successor, proposes an initial step. He believes NATO countries should discuss among themselves their respective difficulties in an effort to present a common diplomatic front to the rest of the world. And he applied this by his own masterly handling of the Cyprus dispute. Only if the alliance were unable to find a solution would it then, Spaak feels, be understandable to "demand the arbitration of another organization," like the U.N. The same would be true for Iceland's disputes on fish exports or France's difficulties in North Africa.

NATO's success as a military alliance forces it to expand its mandate to survive. Today, thanks to adroit Soviet tactics, it is just as urgent that NATO produce a formula for diplomatic defense through consultation and co-operation as it was a few years ago to pool its armed forces. Mere reports to the alliance

Council from the Big Three foreign ministers when they meet with their Soviet counterpart are not sufficient.

The means exist for developing NATO into an operable political alliance. Its permanent secretariat already has a trained set of technical and diplomatic experts at its disposal. This could provide impartial working committees to investigate and analyze any problem. The North Atlantic Council—which includes foreign, defense, and finance ministers—has adopted the custom of meeting every few months. Why does not this machinery go to work?

The Russians have a technical advantage in their coalition; it is a monolith, directed from the top, politically as well as militarily. But the democracies have already shown they can resolve differences and voluntarily unite their armed forces. It is imperative that they develop similar habits on political problems.

There are two final aspects of our relationships with NATO. The first concerns those military bases made available to us by our allies. The second involves the legal status of American soldiers serving overseas.

A primary aim of United States diplomacy during the next few years must be the retention of existing bases abroad and the constant negotiation of accords to modernize such facilities. In this shrinking world in which man flies so fast that he threatens to smash himself in a great rear-end collision, we can only protect ourselves and our allies by continual use of each other's geography.

Military techniques are continuing to evolve. The day may come, during the next decade, when our defenses can be founded on American soil, with some hundred intercontinental-missile installations, and on American ships wandering about the seven seas. But for an indeterminate period prior to that time, we must rely on the intermediate-range-rocket bases we are now constructing overseas in countries as far removed as England and Formosa and on airfields spanning the peripheries of Europe, Africa, and Asia.

Maintenance of this extensive system is both financially costly and diplomatically delicate. While we have bestowed roughly one billion dollars in military and economic aid on Spain, it was in reality a pay-off for the right to build bases.

The problems inherent in securing such privileges are a major concern of both the State Department and the Pentagon. A study of these problems has been made by one of our more brilliant young officers, Colonel Edwin F. Black, in what he terms *A Primer for U.S. Base Negotiators.* He points out that there are two new aspects. The first is increased sensitivity of all lands on matters affecting national sovereignty. The second is development of nuclear weapons, which, as Communist propaganda points out, makes host countries assume greatly enlarged risks in granting us military facilities. He argues: "The concept of exclusive U.S. use of bases is rapidly becoming obsolete. It smacks too much of extra-territoriality to survive for long in the present political climate. Furthermore, in these atomic and thermonuclear times the very presence of a base involves a definite sharing of the defense responsibility by the host country.

"This being the case, it seems foolish on our part to refuse to recognize this fact and to cling to the outmoded idea of exclusive use. How much wiser it would be to begin moving toward the joint use of these bases and to accept now a much greater degree of joint consultation and joint planning with our allies than we have seen fit to permit in the past. In the current period of change and uncertainty, it is a fact that our allies are often more concerned over what we will do next than they are over the Communists' next move. The presence of our overseas bases provides physical proof of our military capability to react at once to an attack. Their absence creates doubts as to the sincerity of our defense commitments."

On the basis of such sensible assumptions, Black concludes: "Once we recognize that we are in a period of historical change, we have, in effect, accepted the principle of the need for modernization of our relationships with our allies. Contracts and agreements previously entered into should be reviewed and brought up-to-date. It should be the United States who takes the initiative in such a revision. We should not, when we intend to make concessions anyway, let ourselves be put in the position of being forced into them or of making these concessions grudgingly. We should get ahead of events."

This is sound advice. It might well be contemplated by those of our diplomatists who are now engaged in NATO-base negotiations.

Finally, there is the complex status of our soldiers' rights at law while they serve abroad in peacetime. On this matter Congress has been far less sensible than the State Department. Not least of the problems presented to us when we suddenly became a superpower with global commitments was the question of United States legal responsibilities to its own citizens stationed abroad in the national interest.

Washington seeks, and quite properly, to dodge pretensions to extraterritorial rights for Americans living in other countries. Such privileges smack of the "imperialism" that we would at all costs avoid. Likewise, we cannot agree to give foreigners dwelling on our soil any particular legal protection to which we at home are not also entitled.

This reasonable philosophy was behind the approach of both the Truman and Eisenhower administrations to the question of "status of forces" treaties. These govern rights and obligations of United States servicemen stationed overseas and of allied troops training in our territory. Such agreements admit primary jurisdiction of the host country to try before its own courts foreign soldiers accused of violating its civil or criminal codes.

What is not generally appreciated is that, technically,

neither signatory party yields any concession. Sovereign states have authority over all lawbreakers within their borders. This is accepted international custom. However, during wars our courts-martial applied to American soldiers abroad. We have sought to adjust to peacetime conditions. This makes our servicemen breaking the law of other lands subject to local courts. Similarly, a foreign pilot training at one of our airfields is responsible to our federal and state laws. Naturally, far more American citizens are garrisoned in allied countries than vice versa.

It is theoretically accepted that a soldier infringing upon some statute while in the course of normal duties or upon his normal base shall be tried by regular American military law. In by far the greatest percentage of cases involving our servicemen abroad, the local government waives jurisdiction in favor of United States military justice.

The intricacy of these relationships between our citizens and the legal systems of other nations has come very much to the fore. In Taiwan there was the unfortunate case of Master Sergeant Reynolds, who was whisked off to Manila before a howling mob. In Japan there was the problem of Army Specialist Girard, who accidentally killed a Japanese woman.

Even in Washington the issue has been raised. The Supreme Court decided that our military tribunals may not try American civilians for certain crimes committed abroad. It ordered the release of two women convicted of murdering their soldier husbands. This inspired the British Ambassador to ask that an Englishwoman, married to an American, be likewise released from prison for a crime committed while she and her husband were in Eritrea at a U.S. installation.

Many well-intentioned Americans, including legislators and members of patriotic organizations, are emotionally opposed to any "status of forces" agreement which could subject our citizens to foreign prisons. Their arguments are generally based on two contentions: that tribunals abroad often apply legal systems we do not consider just; that foreign jails are inferior. The Defense Department has investigated the application to our servicemen of foreign justice. It concluded this was both fair and lenient. There have been complaints at home that eight of our NATO allies, with whom we have "status of forces" covenants, base their laws upon the Napoleonic Code. According to common—if erroneous—belief, this presumes a man guilty until proven innocent. Actually the code was based upon careful study of our own Constitution and Bill of Rights. It remains the foundation for the state laws of Louisiana. The question of jails is vaguer. A criminal in Denmark might be better housed than in Mississippi; in Turkey he would be worse off.

The main point is not to be obscured by technical disputes. Nor can it be measured by bland chauvinism of the type which insists that American boys "protecting" foreign lands should be above local law. The point is that we station troops abroad and make alliances not merely to aid other lands. In so doing we also help ourselves.

As the world shrinks and as our own position in it expands, we must reconsider concepts concerning the rights of our citizenry and those of other nations when they come into sharp contact at home or overseas. Both "status of forces" agreements and the Supreme Court decision emphasize the need for new legal interpretations to handle these developing relationships.

But, in contemplating the problem, we must remember one salient fact. We cannot request legal privileges for our citizens from friends and allies that we are not in turn prepared to grant their subjects. No other country will humiliate itself by voluntarily according us extraterritorial rights that we ourselves are unready to concede.

Let us not forget that one factor that helped to doom NATO's only predecessor, the Delian League, was Athens' insistence that its soldiers, in the event of altercations with allied citizens, should be tried by Athenian courts.

Chapter 6

Chaos and Confusion in the Middle East

The most brilliant and effective foreign-policy stratagem of the Soviet Union has been to appear to associate its own aspirations with those of the newly independent lands in Africa and Asia. The colonialist revolution, which owes its philosophical genesis more to Woodrow Wilson than to Lenin, has roughly coincided in time with the Communist revolution. And, by appearing to sponsor it, Moscow has gained immeasurable advantage in the continuing contest for world power.

The vast area affected, could it ever be dominated by a single coalition, would give that coalition unquestionable paramountcy. It contains the majority of the globe's population, many of its most valuable raw materials, such as tin, rubber, and, above all, petroleum, and the geographical advantages of traditional sea and air routes.

The connecting link between Africa and Asia, using Egypt as a fulcrum, extends across what we call the Middle East. This is a vague if familiar term invented by German geopoliticians. It has come loosely to synonymize both the "Arab world," a region that reaches from Morocco on the Atlantic seacoast to the frontiers of Iran, and a vague cartographical expression that generally includes the countries lying between Libya and India, among them non-Arab Turkey and Iran.

153

While there may be disagreement as to precise definitions of
the phrase, there is no disagreement concerning the importance of the Middle East. Marshal Lyautey, the great
French Arabist who "pacified" Morocco, likened the Arab
world to a drum. When you tapped one end, he said, it boomed
all over.

Russia, as a nation, has sought to extend its influence into
this general area for decades. In fact, the nineteenth- and
twentieth-century Russian penetration of the Caucasus and
Turkestan was merely the beginning of a dynamic process
not yet ended. And early bolshevik dogma, by expounding a
method of aiding oppressed peoples to shake off the imperial
rule that then prevailed, helped Moscow to elaborate the present policy.

Russian aspirations in the Middle East are certainly not new.
Politically they date from Czarist times. Molotov explained
them in meticulous detail to Hitler's Foreign Minister Joachim
von Ribbentrop during a period Moscow would like to forget.
The Soviet Foreign Minister displayed much greed in the
direction of the Mediterranean (via Turkey) and the Persian
Gulf (via Iran). Nor is there anything new in Communism's
ideological concern with this region. Party tactics to be employed were set forth with clarity by Lenin in June 1920. Nothing now occurring in the stretch between Afghanistan and
Morocco would indicate that Lenin's teachings have been
abandoned. In brief, this is what he advocated:

"All the Communist parties must assist the bourgeois-democratic liberation movement in these countries . . . it is
necessary to wage a determined struggle against painting the
bourgeois-democratic liberation trend in backward countries
in Communist colors." And, finally, "the Communist International" (later replaced by the Cominform) "must enter into a
temporary alliance with bourgeois democracy in colonial and
backward countries, but must not merge with it."

Such is the ideological strategy at present applied by Communism in Afghanistan, Egypt, Algeria, Tunisia, Iraq, and Morocco. It permits Nasser, for example, to lock up his local Communists while cozily nuzzling up to Moscow. In no sense, furthermore, can North Africa's "democratic liberation trend" justifiably be depicted in "Communist colors." And the foolish agitation in northwest Pakistan, where the Fakir of Ipi, financed by Afghanistan and Russia, hopes to establish a Pathan state, has no traceable Marxist connection.

Nevertheless, these disparate movements are of interest to the Soviet Union. We cannot complain of this. The U.S.S.R. is one of the world's two superpowers. Like the United States, it hopes to improve its position by making friends and influencing people. There is little sense carping at the methods employed. In point of fact, they are often more skillful than our own.

The question is how to prevent an uneasy area, deeply injected with fanaticism and xenophobia, from turning wholeheartedly against the West. The means so far chosen have not been entirely sensible.

As stated earlier, the United States has placed too much reliance on pacts. In 1953, Dulles suggested the alliance called the Northern Tier, which included Turkey, Iran, Pakistan, Britain, and Iraq. This was a virtual failure from the start. All it succeeded in accomplishing was to encourage Moscow to leapfrog over it to Cairo.

Likewise, we reacted to London's stimulus and helped form the Southeast Asian coalition called SEATO, the Southeast Asia Treaty Organization. This also includes Pakistan. Thus, through Pakistan, the Soviet bloc's southern frontier is nicely sealed off on the map all the way from the Mediterranean to the South China Sea. Unfortunately, although this may look impressive to a child with a geography book, it really does not signify much. Pakistan is unreal as now constituted. Its two halves are separated by a thousand miles of India, which has been rendered unnecessarily hostile by our alliance with its

enemy. SEATO has little effective meaning. Britain and its
Dominions continue to build Southeast Asian defenses only
at the Kra Isthmus, just north of Malaya.

The fallacy of the Northern Tier has already been demonstrated by Moscow's arms deals in the Middle East. And it is
questionable that the alliance can even survive the revolution in Iraq. Pacts that are mere map-making exercises rarely
endure. Those that depend on one man—as the Northern
Tier did, to a large extent, on the murdered Premier
Nuri-as-Said—are wobbly. Policy in the Middle East can never
be firmly based upon individuals. Israel found that out when
negotiating a secret peace with Jordan's King Abdullah. Abdullah was assassinated—and with him Israeli hopes of peace.

Such considerations should be weighed seriously now that
we are re-examining our Middle Eastern posture. The problems are so massive that they have not even been properly
defined. They are complicated by almost insuperable
economic and social illnesses. The area involved is being
hoisted suddenly from prefeudal depths into the atomic age.
No wonder it has the bends.

We have been astonishingly imperceptive and ill-informed
on Middle Eastern matters. This condition dates back to before the war. There is a tale, which I cannot prove, that, at
the Casablanca conference in 1943, we made a curious deal
with the British. Roosevelt very much wanted his slogan of
"unconditional surrender," so familiar to any American, accepted as the basis for Allied intentions. Churchill and his principal lieutenants objected. They felt this would force the Germans to fight on until the end, protracting hostilities unnecessarily. The story, as I have heard it, is that Churchill
made a secret arrangement with the President. He agreed to
endorse "unconditional surrender" if, in exchange, we ac-
corded him strategic control of the eastern Mediterranean
area, including the Balkans and the Middle East. So secret
was this arrangement between the two great leaders that even

Secretary of State Cordell Hull was unaware of it. In 1944, when we began to send our first military and transport shipments to Turkey, Lord Halifax (then ambassador in Washington) is said to have protested to Hull: "This violates the Casablanca compact because it was not first cleared with us." "What compact?" asked Hull.

In any case, whether this is correct or not, we assuredly did not prepare for postwar conditions in the Middle East any more farsightedly than we prepared for postwar conditions elsewhere. Consequently, in the Middle East, where we had little practical diplomatic experience, our views were utterly confused for many years. And we have been hampered by a paucity of first-class minds familiar with the area's intricacies.

Furthermore, our policy has been warped by local politics. Thus, in 1945, Truman, seeking to aid Democrats in a New York City election, publicly demanded a sudden increase in Jewish immigration to Palestine. This came when Arab and Zionist representatives were secretly negotiating in London. It upset the course of talks.

Following Israel's establishment and the Palestine armistice, we developed the idea of an alliance which eventually became the Baghdad Pact. But, after fathering it, we crippled this entente by refusing to join.

We sought to curry Arab favor by pressing Britain to evacuate its Suez military base. Yet we failed to consider all the consequences of that decision.

We fumbled Nasser's arms requests, and he turned to the Soviet bloc. But we did not—despite urgings from Ambassador Henry A. Byroade, beginning in August 1955—attempt to devise means of facing what would be a grave new situation.

From September 1955, it was evident that Israel was seriously considering armed action before Egypt became too strong. That October, Premier David Ben-Gurion argued to me confidentially: "If it turns out to be true that the Egyptians are receiving between eighty and 100 MIGs, as reported, we will have to smash them." He thought this could be done without full-scale war. We refused to comprehend this threat and continued to place reliance upon platitudinous assurances of neutrality and desire for peace—plus faith in U.N. machinery already demonstrably inadequate.

Our policy in the Middle East was simply not clear enough to ourselves to enable us to make it clear to others. Thus, we could not warn in advance of the probable repercussions, as far as we were concerned, of any ill-considered actions.

Britain and France irked us and, in a very real sense, betrayed our confidence when they moved against Egypt and brought the world to disaster's desperate edge. But we cannot escape the fact that befuddled lack of planning helped us lose control of situations where our interests are vital. And our allies pushed the whole world to a terrifying threshold when we insisted, while offering no substitute, on keeping them upon the brink of a Middle Eastern peace which did not even then, in reality, exist. It is said that when Dulles first learned in 1955 that Moscow was unloading arms in the Middle East he had a "conniption fit." From a human standpoint this is understandable. The Secretary of State had been giving a passable imitation of Sisyphus rolling the rock of peace up Levantine slopes. It was surely no pleasure to be shoved down by the Kremlin.

Yet no diplomatist should have been surprised by developments. Soviet interest in the Arab world has little to do with ideology. Since the eighteenth century, Russia has been pressing toward Iran, Turkey, and the eastern Mediterranean and laying claim to special rights in Palestine. Years ago it was already clear that commissarist tactics were following Czarist patterns. The Russians were admitted to the international committee governing Moroccan Tangier—although remaining inactive. They laid claim, during preliminary peace talks, to ports in Italian Libya and Eritrea.

With this background it is not astonishing to find Moscow

insisting on a share in Middle Eastern destinies. Only in 1956, a publication called *Palestinski Sbornik* reappeared in the U.S.S.R. That issue was No. 63. The other sixty-two were printed before the revolution.

Ever since the Afro-Asian Bandung conference in 1955, Soviet interest in the Arab world has been mounting—partly to offset Communist China's growing prestige. Nasser went twice to Russia. Commercial exchanges between the area and the Soviet bloc expanded. It was to be expected that Cairo and Moscow would draw nearer to each other as our own policy worked against them both. The Northern Tier alliance sponsored by us is equally offensive to Moscow and Cairo. Khrushchev regards it as a threat to his southern border. Nasser saw in it an effort to build Iraqi influence over that of Egypt.

The Geneva summit conference, from a Russian point of view, accomplished two things. It insured that no power was prepared at present to start atomic war. And it froze, *de facto,* Europe's prevailing political frontiers. Moscow thus felt free to turn its attentions more energetically to the Middle East.

We know and it is safe to assume the Russians know that peddling arms in the Middle East is dangerous. A sudden explosion there would be more conducive to atomic world war than any peninsular conflict in Korea or Indochina. Why, then, is Moscow rocking the boat? The answer appears fairly obvious, if difficult for us to digest. First of all, Russia has managed at last to assert itself as a recognized great power in the Middle East. Secondly, it is plain the Soviets desire a share in Middle Eastern developments and wealth. Thirdly, they wish to neutralize the area. And fourthly, they hope to threaten NATO from a new quarter.

Were the Middle East ever to associate itself with the Soviet bloc, it would be a greater blow to the United States than was the communization of China. Europe's petroleum resources and much of our own reserve are located there. The Mediterranean's south coast would be lost and NATO outflanked.

Moscow seeks to win the area by arms deals, economic penetration, and diplomacy. And Russian technicians have now swarmed into the Nile and Euphrates valleys. The West, facing these threats, has not yet devised any clear-cut answer. But there is no single clear-cut answer, now that the ill-advised Suez expedition ended in fiasco and an almost split alliance. When we, by shortsighted methods, sought to forestall possible Soviet military penetration, we facilitated political penetration. And we lost the sympathies of Egypt, node of the Arab world.

Outstanding problems concerning us in the Middle East include the need for Palestine peace, for resolving allied disunity, for counteracting Soviet penetration, and, finally, Egypt's claim to Arab leadership.

But Palestine alone could be insoluble. Arab public declarations insist Israel must disappear. Many Arabs are prepared to wait a century if necessary to achieve this. And are we at last ready to swallow our pride and acknowledge Egypt's regional leadership claims? Would we, for example, envision Cairo as central headquarters for a Middle Eastern Marshall Plan?

There are, in fact, two doctrines today contesting the fate of the Middle East. The first is the Eisenhower Doctrine, which has proven ineffective because it is designed to meet only an improbable and outmoded threat of direct aggression. The second is the Khrushchev doctrine based on Lenin's 1920 speech. Khrushchev and his colleagues are proving the excellence of their Leninism. Throughout the Middle East, "liberation" movements and "bourgeois-democratic" nationalism are in "temporary alliance" with Communism.

Precisely as the Eisenhower Doctrine sought to do, the Khrushchev doctrine employs both economic and military aid to pursue its aims. The Eisenhower Doctrine tried to erect a horizontal barrier along the U.S.S.R.'s borders in order to block Soviet southward penetration. Khrushchev endeavors to create a vertical axis running from Russia down to Cairo. Ultimately, this would incorporate the Kurds of northern Iran and Iraq and eastern Turkey; plus Syria, Jordan, and Egypt.

The Eisenhower Doctrine found itself frustrated in trying to compose the explosive Palestine question without favoring one side over the other. Khrushchev seeks to decompose it, while avoiding precise commitments. As Turkey observed in a 1957 report to NATO: "Moscow, while exploiting the various manifestations of the Israeli problem, shirks from taking a definite stand as regards the core of the problem. Thus on the one hand, it prefers not to adopt a clear position for the settlement of the Israeli question—which in any case it prefers to see remain open. On the other, it tries to exploit fully Arab antagonism towards Israel and, by rebound, towards the West; also the miserable state of Arab refugees. The second of these weapons has certainly been the most advantageous element for Communist penetration in the Middle East, notably in Jordan, Syria and Lebanon."

The difficulty of the Eisenhower Doctrine when it confronted the Khrushchev doctrine was to avoid overemphasizing military aspects while insuring that Middle Eastern nations are capable of maintaining internal security and mounting at least minimal defenses. Moscow feeds just enough weapons into the restless area to make acutely difficult our job of balancing arms and economic aid.

Prince Naim, Afghanistan's Foreign Minister, who is sympathetic to our doctrine's objectives, told me in Kabul in 1957: "Not one of the countries in the Middle East can erect a defense against a big modern power. The most effective weapon in our part of the world is to achieve a better standard of living. This would do more than any military equipping of any country to preserve its independence. A big army is a great burden even for a large and prosperous power."

The Eisenhower Doctrine is now virtually a dead letter. Nevertheless, it is certainly essential that we give friendly Middle Eastern governments sufficient strength to protect themselves against subversive *coups d'état*. Furthermore, it is in our own interest to safeguard any emergency bases they may afford us or our allies. But beyond that flexible limit it is probably even harmful to try to build their military establishments and thus increase their economic burden. The Russians may see that pitfall facing us. It costs them little to unload obsolescent weapons in the Levant to keep the area on a brink of war. It is, therefore, unfortunate that when Moscow proposed discussion of an end to this regional munitions race we did not isolate that single promising suggestion from the mass of propaganda in which it was embedded—and try to negotiate on it.

The basic problems of the Middle East are misery, chaos, and emotionalism; water-sharing, education, and hygiene; protection of free legitimate access to mineral wealth and transit routes; and, above all, peace in Palestine. Arms shipments cannot solve them.

We never had a basic Middle Eastern policy prior to World War II. Immediately after the peace, we faced the problem created by dynamic Zionism. This, with considerable American aid, resulted in the establishment of Israel and an Arab-Jewish war not yet over. But, despite evident emotional imbalance in the Middle East and despite its blatantly outdated social system, we seemed strangely convinced we could guide it along the path of comfortable, reformist evolution. We failed to recognize the regional challenge of Russia.

We were misled by false shibboleths. We assumed that because Russia had previously tried to reach the Mediterranean and failed, it would again not manage to intrude. We regarded the religious fervor of Islam as built-in insurance against the appeal of Communism. We forgot that the U.S.S.R. is an important Moslem power with a large Mohammedan population from which agents could be drawn.

In 1949 a Congressional subcommittee published a report on Communist strategy which tended to echo State Department wishful thinking. This said: "A careful appraisal of the situation in the Near East . . . indicates that communism, either through its official and unofficial agents or its ideology, presents no serious danger of immediate Communist control. . . . Nothing in the history of the peoples (of the Middle East) is particularly conducive toward receptivity to Communist propaganda."

This was a shortsighted and erroneous view—and one for which we shall continue to pay until we recast our assumptions. It forgets four things:

(1) Since it came to power, Soviet leadership has sought to encourage nationalism in former colonial areas without seeking to assert Communist control of such movements—in fact, while disassociating Communism from them.

(2) A power vacuum was created in the Middle East when the British, who had ruled largely from India, and the French could no longer fill it. The United States was unwilling and unable to. Meanwhile, Russia became a dynamic empire on the area's border.

(3) With the withdrawal of Anglo-Indian and French authority, the seeds of nationalism first planted by Wilson and nourished by Soviet Russia had a chance to sprout.

(4) The social and economic structure of the region is rotten and ripe for revolution.

But even if we had properly analyzed these ideas, we would have been hampered in dealing with them. We are allied with the British, French, and Turks, who are detested for memories of past oppression. Our missionaries have been at least as preoccupied with converting Moslems as in educating them—which leads to resentment. And the wealth brought in by our oil companies has not been distributed to the impoverished masses.

A glance at statistics shows how desperately social change is needed. In 1956, less than 1 per cent of the population of Saudi Arabia attended school, while perhaps 10 per cent of the population were chattel slaves. Right after the war there were only four secondary schools in Jordan. Two years ago Aden's infant mortality rate was 156 for every 1,000 births. This condition was not rectified by distributing huge petroleum royalties to sheikhs and emirs to build palaces and embellish harems.

We did not remember that no true geographical frontiers existed in the Middle East. Syria, Lebanon, Iraq, and Jordan were created with artificially imposed borders after two world wars. Israel's boundaries are not yet firmly acknowledged. The structure of British colonies and protectorates along Arabia's southeast shore is tottering.

Such factors lend themselves to the attraction of passionate Pan-Arab nationalism. And there is no necessary cleavage between such a concept and Moscow's orthodox doctrine. Marx said: "A nation is an historically evolved, stable community of language, territory, economic life and psychological make-up manifested in a community of culture." Stability is what the Arabs lack; but not the other qualifications.

There are many internal conflicting forces in the Levant. However, most of these are dynastic and tribal. There is a broad community of language and Koranic culture. There is territorial contiguity. And there is a common urge to cast off shackles of a feudal past. All these elements should be recognized as we prepare to formulate our policy for the area.

Finally, we must never forget the highly charged quality of the Arab people. As long ago as 1950 Abd-el-Krim el Khatabi, Emir of the Riff, who fought the French and Spaniards thirty years earlier, warned me: "Soon we may be obliged to fight again against France and Spain. We will count only upon ourselves. We are distant from the Communist ideology, which is a danger to the Arabs and Moslems. We must achieve independence by our own means. But if in our struggle the situation becomes critical, we would gladly accept arms or support from any quarter—even Moscow."

The man who expresses this threat in by far the most significant way is Nasser, the hero of the new Arab nationalism. Nasser's importance is not that he represents any novel ideology. He is the symptom of a historic tide, not its moving force. He does not inspire events, he reacts to them.

Even Nasser admits he did not arrange his union with Syria as the result of careful advance planning. "We lost the initiative," he told me in 1958. "Public opinion forced the union on us." This is only partly true; for Nasser is an able underground conspirator. "There were ten parties in Syria," he said. "Their leaders came to me saying everything was a mess. I met with all except the Communists. They told me: 'Only you can save us. Liquidate our parties and join us to Egypt.' "

Those sentiments which prompted federation were inspired primarily by xenophobia. Egypt and Syria dislike the West. They regard America as Israel's main crutch. Our alliance with the area's former imperial masters links us to their hated past. And our intentions are distorted by a deliberately hostile press.

But agitation alone cannot build solidly on the Levant's shifting political sands. Administrative experience is in short supply. Nasser himself confided to me: "We don't have planning committees and maps on the walls which say what is to be the Arab federation of the future. It is our policy to have flexibility. We don't have any detailed program."

The future of Nasser's ideology is uncertain. He talks vaguely of restoring multiparty democracy in about five years. But that dictator who voluntarily returns power to the people is a rare bird. Nasser is unpredictable for the simple reason he himself does not know what he wishes to do. As he extends his power he endeavors to improve his political education. His desk is piled with books whose ideas are not yet digested.

A fervent orator, which is essential for any Arab leader, Nasser exerts almost mystical mass appeal, but he is lacking in practical concepts. He is both the product of and spokesman for the winter of Arab discontent. He did not originate the movement which now is changing the face of the Middle East. He was created by it and became its leading symbol. If he should disappear, other "Nassers" would aspire to his role.

Nasser is no Communist. His only ideology is that of improvisation. But his attitude toward Moscow for too long seemed one of uncritical admiration, until the Russians gained a toe hold in Iraq. The Egyptian dictator, who now exercises absolute control over Syria and dominates Yemen, is a devout Mohammedan. Nevertheless, the boastful atheism of Soviet credo either eludes or fails to impress him. He prefers not to believe that the Kremlin squashes Islam in Soviet Central Asia. He says: "Remember, there are less than ten million members of the Communist party in Russia. Those people must follow the religious philosophy of Marx. But others have liberty to believe. This is what I am told.

"There is absolutely no problem between the Soviet Union and Egypt," Nasser happily observes. "They have helped us greatly. They helped us with war supplies. When we faced great economic pressures and really needed aid, they gave it. Our money was frozen in Britain and America; so we asked Russia for petroleum. They agreed at once. When you refused to supply us with wheat, they did. When we asked for a loan, they lent us 200,000,000 rubles. And there are no ties. They haven't made a single political request. It may seem strange; but that's what happened—no single political request. We asked for much help—and they were agreeable. Your newspapers write of trouble in our relations with Moscow. That is nonsense. You Americans say aggression will come from there. Should there be such aggression, we would expect Western help. But what about aggression from the West? We would ask for Soviet assistance. The West says such aggression is impossible. Eden told me this himself in 1955. But what happened? One year later he joined France and Israel to attack us."

When accused of Communist sympathies, Nasser is furious. "If you say I am putting Egypt under Communist domination, that is unfair," he complains. "If you say I'm taking orders from Russia or playing the West against the East, that is unfair. If you say I'm a Communist, that's untrue. If you say we work for Russia, that hurts our dignity."

Nasser does not pretend Egypt's Communist party was banned because it is Marxist; only because all parties are illegal. The same, says he, applies to newly absorbed Syria. He does not assert the United Arab Republic was established to prevent Syria from going Communist. He insists this never entered into his calculations. Indeed, he is never less than fulsome about his Soviet friends. The chief of the new United Arab Republic believes in nonalignment. But this, at least until the Iraqi coup, was clearly nonalignment with an Eastern bias. Nasser's attitude has been a handsome dividend on the policy laid down by Lenin three decades ago.

But the danger to all concerned, including the Russians and ourselves, is that Nasser's military ambitions (coddled by Moscow) may eventually bring disaster to the world. Apart from his fears of Israel, enhanced by that country's alliance with Britain and France during the Suez war, the Egyptian dictator has a curious reason for constantly seeking weapons supplies.

In 1955 he told me his only political support came from the Egyptian army; without this support he would be unable to carry out the social and economic aims to which he aspired. Therefore, he reasoned, Egypt's army must at all costs be satisfied in order to continue the revolution. "What is the meaning of friendship?" he asked. "For the army it is equipment. The army is a basic factor in Egyptian life. Our revolution was stimulated in the army by a lack of equipment. If our officers feel we still have no equipment, they will lose faith in the government."

Nasser complained: "We are asked if we intend to use our equipment against Israel. I reply that I am not interested in waging war. I want to build up my country. I want to raise the standard of living."

"But," I observed to him, "you cannot sow cotton from a jet plane. You cannot draw plows behind tanks."

We have not for long been in the habit of looking ahead diplomatically in many regions of the world. Neither the approaching collapse of the British and French Levantine empires, nor the expression of Zionism, nor the rise of Arab nationalism, nor the discovery of ever-increasing oil deposits, had yet brought the Middle East to Washington's serious attention until World War II.

Although we had had business, educational, and missionary contacts in that area for decades, our government was projected into it highly unprepared. In the role of superpower, we became abruptly charged with immense responsibilities.

Furthermore, we injected ourselves into by far the most explosive Middle Eastern problem by our enthusiastic advocacy of Israel's creation. Not only did American Jews send millions of dollars to the Zionist movement, but arms and even military experts were privately furnished. And the Democratic administration, quite obviously courting Jewish votes, committed Washington to a position of outright support of Israel. This, even though slightly toned down, remains the attitude of the Republican administration. Therefore, we are directly a party to the most flaming dispute within the Arab world.

In the Middle East, we can discern a sufficient difference in emphasis to say that the Eisenhower foreign policy differs substantially from that of Truman. For example, it has chosen to develop ties with Pakistan at the risk of courting hostility in India. And there has been less tendency to favor Israel over the Middle Eastern Arab states.

If basic United States policy has not altered its long-range implications, nevertheless the surface emphasis is changed. We recognize the immense importance of India in blocking Communism in the East. We admit that no useful economic organization for free Asia could succeed without Indian participation. At Asia's western extremity we retain much interest in Israel. But there is no longer any tendency to overvalue what Sir Oliver Franks, former British Ambassador in Washington, used to refer to as a New Delhi-Tel Aviv axis.

The reason for this changed emphasis was political stultification in the Middle East. No plan for devising potential area protection against external aggression or internal subversion seemed to stand a chance. The proposed Middle East Defense Organization to complement NATO never advanced beyond the blueprint stage. Washington's scheme for parallel security pacts with the Arab states and Israel failed. Moslem fanaticism, directed against both Israel and the Anglo-American bloc, combined with pandering to uninformed and hysterical opinion by the Middle Eastern governments. The result was stalemate.

Washington then sought to terminate the diplomatic impasse that prevailed after the first Palestine war. By two endeavors, it tried to focus the attention of the Arab states northward toward Soviet Russia and the danger of direct or indirect aggression; and it attempted to focus Egypt's attention away from Western Asia and southward into Africa.

Both of these rather awkward efforts failed signally. They were not coherently conceived, adequately presented, or harmonized with our suspicious European allies. And, in the meantime, our original legacy of popularity waned to the verge of zero.

The cancer of the Palestine war eats deeply into efforts at benevolence. Suspicions of colonialism rankle among the newly independent peoples. And the United States, as the most powerful nation of the West, is suspected of new-fashioned imperialism no matter what we seek to accomplish. Fear and deep-seated complexes distort Middle Eastern views of America. Israel, frightened of the hostile Arab masses, blames us for arming its enemies. Egypt claims we give weapons only to opponents of Arab welfare. And throughout the area, revolutionary movements look increasingly toward the Communist bloc to solve their troubles.

When Iran, under the eccentric Mohammed Mossadegh, almost collapsed, Washington intensified its concern with the Middle East. The Truman administration began to conceive regional policies along lines Eisenhower would surely have defined later as in our own "enlightened self-interest." We joined Britain and France in abortive efforts to establish a Middle East defense organization.

Privately, we encouraged London and Cairo to reach agreement on the Suez Canal base. Before the Suez settlement and while the Anglo-Egyptian quarrel continued, Pakistan requested our support for her projected alliance with Turkey. We agreed. From this developed the Northern Tier defense pact of states along the Soviet border.

This arrangement provoked a storm. Israel objected to our giving weapons to her enemy Iraq. Egypt was angry that the Arab League's political unity had been shattered. Cairo contended we were seeking to split, isolate, and dominate the Arab states to force them into peace with Jerusalem. Advisers of Nasser told him Iraq was planning to federate with Syria and form a great state with Jordan under the Hashemite dynasty; that such a power would threaten Egypt.

Nasser and his Revolution Command Council—a sort of nonideological Politburo—have been reared in an atmosphere of conspiracy and suspicion. They concluded we were trying to strengthen Israel, create an anti-Egyptian Hashemite state, stir up trouble to the south in the Sudan, and apply pressure from Libya to the west—in one clever diabolical scheme. Egypt, therefore, started a countermove. This developed into union with Syria, affiliation with Yemen, and uncharted further aspirations. It solicited and received Soviet support, at least until Moscow began to toy with the idea of a puppet Iraq.

We are in a diplomatically impossible position as long as the Palestine issue remains unsettled. And there is no sign of approaching peace. Israel complains whenever we aid the Arabs, who in turn suspect we encourage Israeli pugnacity.

When I first met him, in 1955, Nasser naïvely assured me that until rather lately he had always thought all Communists were "thieves." But at Bandung, he found he liked the amiable Chou En-lai. There he also met and liked the affable Dmitri Shepilov, then secretary of the Bolshevik Central Committee, but now in Soviet disgrace. And he discovered he could trade with Russia and purchase arms.

The Arabs began to wonder if, after all, the Soviet Union would not prove a better friend than the mistrusted West. And we distributed arms instead of wisdom. Some of those arms were later used to assassinate our three best friends in Iraq. We backed Nasser. But we would not give him all the weapons he demanded; so he turned to Russia.

Because we unnecessarily offended the Egyptian dictator, we provoked him into seizing the Suez Canal Company. This event could have been foreseen in the cloudiest crystal ball. But we were caught totally unprepared. When Britain and France, together with Israel, cooked up a war to defend vital interests similar to those we now help London protect, we scotched their plan. Thanks to us, Nasser was rescued from disaster and built to hero's stature.

If our policy was correct in 1956 when we backed Cairo against Paris and London, it was incorrect in 1958 when we joined Britain in the Jordan-Lebanon expedition. Certainly the 1958 Anglo-American intervention came at the wrong places, at the wrong time, for the wrong reasons. At least Anthony Eden and Guy Mollet had reason on their side when they went for Suez.

We did not rush troops to Lebanon because of a sudden turn in that country's operetta insurrection. Iraq was the real explanation. Yet, when we got our troops installed, we reversed field and recognized the new Iraqi government. And Jordan, again insured by Britain, is not a nation at all. A map-maker's dream, it was created by Churchill and T. E. Lawrence over brandy and cigars to pay a feudal debt.

Nasser was taking kindergarten lessons on Soviet imperialism from Tito when we landed in Lebanon. Just as he was becoming wary, we drove him back to Khrushchev's arms.

The resulting mishmash cannot possibly be stabilized where it now is. No matter how long Lebanon and Jordan totter along, they will fall between the jaws of a hostile Baghdad-Cairo nutcracker if Moscow can ever draw those two capitals together. Such is the logic of the situation. But logic has rarely featured our Middle Eastern policy.

In the Middle East, Dulles, as he has admitted, considered the situation so changeable that it became difficult even to formulate objectives. Therefore, he operated on a day-to-day and place-to-place basis. Within these loose terms he reckoned on certain assumptions. One was the obvious fact, which he reluctantly conceded, that Nasser has immense popular appeal among the Arabs. Another was the belief that Russia is in no position to take over the area's petroleum interests because the U.S.S.R. has no marketing facilities and is itself an oil exporter. He also assumed that Khrushchev does not intend to call for a return to the 1947 Palestine borders. He calculated the Arabs would not really welcome this. The 1947 settlement awarded all the Negev to Israel, and actually Saudi Arabia and Egypt would like to do away with the Israeli port of Elath there.

For our makeshift decisions we have had to rely upon the reporting of our diplomatic and other representatives in the Levant. This has not always been up to scratch. Washington had no advance inkling of the Iraqi coup. We took days to realize it represented a relatively popular movement. Subsequently, we had to amend original intentions of promoting intervention to overthrow the insurrectional government.

We had been similarly ill-served before. Less than a fortnight prior to Nasser's first Moscow visit, one of our principal agents was betting that the Egyptian dictator would not go to the Soviet Union that year. When Prince Faisal assumed real power in Saudi Arabia, our Ambassador cabled analyses based on conversations with the Master of the Royal Garage. The United States has few outstanding envoys in an area where we belatedly recognize our interests are vital. Only a handful of them speak Arabic. If we are ever to regain our influence, we must rectify this weakness.

The Middle East is well along in the processes of a great ferment which we cannot stop. The ruler of Kuwait, Britain's most important petroleum appanage, is dickering with Cairo. Hints of trouble extend from Aden across Saudi Arabia to Bahrein and even as far westward as Morocco. Egypt has been sending skilled agitators, teachers, and military advisers to most of the nations of Islam. Their activities are paying off. And Cairo, which has openly engaged in a radio cold war since May 25, 1957, orders its propagandists to sow dissent.

We cannot save the situation by seeking to preserve a *status quo* that never, in fact, existed. Whether we gain the temporary support of artificial regimes or artificial client states, these are not reality. It is obvious from our latest actions that we have decided against the risk of trying to squash Nasser. Such being the case, the disagreeable alternative is to make terms.

In the end we must come to some form of reckoning with the only true force prevailing in the Middle East, that nationalism implied by Nasserism. This is not a Communist movement. We must cease befuddling ourselves with slogans. It is no more Marxist than was Turkey's Kemalist revolt over three decades ago. Unfortunately, the Kremlin has been cleverer than we in using for its own purposes the high political wind that sweeps the lands of Araby.

I hold no brief for Colonel Nasser, nor do I feel that I have succumbed dizzily to those immense charms he has managed to apply to most American visitors with prodigious success.

(He is without doubt, when he wishes so to be, one of the most attractive personalities on the present-day world stage.) On the other hand, neither do I regard Nasser with such bleak, almost religious disapproval as Dulles seems to do. Nasser is a phenomenon with which we must live, an expression of a popular mood in the wide span of Arabia, and he will never be a Communist unless we make him one. Indeed, once (in 1955) he confided to me that the man he admired most was Marshal Tito. "He has taught me how to get help from both sides," said the Egyptian, "without joining either."

But we must recognize the aspirations he stands for and the deeply sensitive pride he represents, the touchiness of people who have been oppressed for centuries by foreigners and therefore deeply suspect others' intentions and take affront at the slightest implication of offense.

The game we have played with Nasser has been acutely clumsy. We backed him enthusiastically at the start of his revolution and eventually sent a young former army officer as ambassador on the theory the two might chat on cozy terms. We endorsed his great project for a Nile dam at Aswan until we became convinced he was playing a Russian game. We abandoned support in a manner calculated to produce maximum resentment. There we succeeded. Rancor, nationalism, and xenophobia prompted Nasser's seizure of the Suez company.

Nasser himself told me that even were the dam to be built on schedule it could not raise national living standards. The Aswan scheme, as now drawn up, would be so costly that one wonders if it is the proper approach to solving Egypt's most perplexing problem—insufficient arable land and a rising population. It is questionable whether Washington should ever have considered helping build it. If we propose to finance white elephants merely to prevent Moscow from so doing, that is not policy; it is asininity.

But our second mistake was the way we reneged. Had Dulles understood the importance of face saving in the emotional Levant, he might merely have pigeonholed the matter, stalling whenever Cairo requested information. Nasser would soon have caught the point—without needless public embarrassment. Instead, Dulles elected to be brutal in his turndown. This, says Jack Beal, the Secretary's authorized biographer, was a deliberate "gambit" designed to force a cold-war issue. That it did.

Dulles is famous for intellectual acrobatics, forceful advocacy of positions, and an avidity for travel. But if thought processes attributed to him are correct, one is forced to consider the conclusion of Callières, which I have already mentioned, that legal training "breeds habits and dispositions of mind which are not favorable to the practice of diplomacy."

After the Suez war, which we halted, we contemplated alternative approaches to Nasser. One was to get tough: to dump cotton in order to force Nasser's collapse; to join the Baghdad Pact; and simultaneously to guarantee Israel with a security treaty. The other was to attempt bribing Cairo again with professions of good will. We have not quite done either. Meanwhile, Nasser's propagandists all over the Levant foment admiration for him and antipathy for us. They present him as military victor over Israel, Britain, and France, and diplomatic victor over us.

When King Saud visited Pakistan prior to his Washington journey, he boasted of Nasser's triumph. The then president, Iskander Mirza, a forthright man, inquired: "What kind of an army wins by losing half its forces? Thirty-eight Egyptian MIGs took refuge on Saudi Arabian airfields. Is that the way to fight? The Israelis could have taken Suez if the British hadn't messed things up. They could have cooked Nasser. And who is trying to upset Your Majesty's dynasty? Nasser. Yet you employ his teachers in your schools. His officers train your army. Does that make sense?" Saud did not sleep all night. But when he went to Washington he heard no such straight talk.

The Suez crisis, between Dulles's blunt reneging on our Aswan promises, Nasser's seizure of the Canal, and the brief, flamboyant war, was an appalling tragicomedy of Western errors. Washington started off by exerting pressure upon Britain and France to forgo the possibility of military force in asserting their national interest in Egypt. Morally, this was without doubt a noble attitude. But diplomatically its validity was never demonstrated. We prevented our two most useful allies from establishing in advance of negotiations a meaningful position of strength—the menace, at least, of belligerent intention. And at the same time we managed, perhaps unwittingly, to undermine British and French public opinion.

We then comforted ourselves that gathering pressures of economic and political logic would induce Nasser to agree to a satisfactory settlement. We felt it was evident the financial and commercial future of Egypt could not develop without our own and Europe's benevolent help. But there was nothing in Nasser's record to support this miscalculation. His statements about the Soviet arms deal, the Aswan Dam, and the reasons for the Suez move were tinged with no sympathy for the West.

Transcending in importance any purely Egyptian attitude was that of the Soviet Union. Moscow plays its own "brink of war" game in the Middle East. It may be demonstrated from the record that as Western bellicosity has waned, that of the U.S.S.R. seems to wax.

Ours is an empirical foreign policy. We seek to deal with crises only as they arise, and then proceed to hope for happy endings. Aware of the implicit terror of war, we hasten not only to forgo its methods in advance of international discussions, but to assure our enemies that we will similarly restrain our only allies capable of exercising such a threat themselves.

This is like giving the opponent in a poker game a good look at your hand and then, if he is impressed, offering him some of your cards before the betting starts.

We rely upon negotiation and the value of persuasion. Such methods are traditional to nonrevolutionary diplomacy and might, in other circumstances, even be acceptable to Egypt. But, in world affairs, the Egyptian revolution is overshadowed by that of the Soviet Union. We wish to perpetuate what is left of a stable world system by compromising disagreements. But the Kremlin has no interest in stability. Even if Nasser wishes a suitable *modus vivendi* with the West—which surely remains to be proved—it is unlikely Moscow would permit it. The U.S.S.R. is in a powerful psychological position in the Middle East. And for Russia everything is to be gained and nothing to be lost by prodding crises away from possible solution. Soviet policy seeks to cripple NATO. There are two excellent avenues of approach. The first is to undercut Europe's economy by choking off its oil supplies. The second is to divide the United States from Britain and France.

Eden, as Prime Minister, cautioned Khrushchev and Bulganin against the first tactic. He warned that London would be prepared to go to war rather than accept it. But we more or less guaranteed to Moscow that such would not be the case. And then we implemented this guarantee by turning against the Suez expedition.

The threat of war is an instrument of diplomatic policy. Dulles himself recognizes the validity of such a technique. He believes that more than once he managed to save the peace by venturing to war's brink. Eden implied this, too, was his formula when he warned Moscow concerning Britain's deep interest in the Middle East. But we removed the teeth from his argument.

Indirectly, between Dulles's Aswan statement and the outbreak of hostilities, we actually, if unconsciously, helped stimulate the Suez conflict. This was a total disaster. Had we refrained from interfering for but seventy-two more hours, such would not have been the case.

And to achieve wholly negative results in their ill-planned 1956 war, Britain and France sacrificed to a considerable degree the moral position of the West. It became far more difficult to advertise abroad the cynical Soviet brutality in Hungary when two powers of the Occident simultaneously struck Egypt.

The philosophical cause of freedom was set back incalculably. Moscow's propaganda busily equated its Hungarian action with the unsuccessful Western war in Egypt. The West had been shown unable, in Eastern Europe, to help those prepared to die for freedom's sake. Then, simultaneously, two of its leading governments indicated willingness still to kick small peoples they dislike.

This is an unsatisfactory reckoning. Had there been a successful swift coup at Suez, history might have been entirely different. In the long run, its recorders could have devised convincing arguments to prove the validity of the Egyptian move. Nothing, indeed, succeeds like success. But nothing also, as is so regrettably remembered by the denizens of Monte Carlo, fails like failure.

When one considers our own relations with Nasser and the other Arab nationalists, one must remember that a fault of United States policy in the Arab world is that we have tended to deal with men outdated by events. Too many of our compacts are with leaders who represent the past more than the future. Our prestige suffers when those whom we back decline in power.

This was the case in Saudi Arabia. We seemed to sponsor the maladroit King Saud. When he shifted real authority back to Emir Faisal, many Arabs assumed this was a blow to us. We were intimately associated with Iraq's Premier Nuri-as-Said. When he was assassinated, many of his enemies proved tinted with anti-Americanism merely because they had been anti-Nuri and saw us as his backer. And elsewhere, in such British controlled or protected areas as Muscat, the Trucial Coast, and Aden, are we torn by the dilemma of loyalty to an ally and readiness to see change? In the Middle East, one deals with established governments. But this does not necessitate appearing to accept outmoded ideas. We need not become entangled too intimately in the Arabs' own cold wars.

Nor can we permit ourselves to oppose the vague but frenetic torrent of Arab nationalism by clumsy handling of Nasser. As an individual, he is difficult for us to deal with, because he is tricky and does not truly know what he wants. He has no precise plan for economic betterment. A conspirator and gambler, he is not averse to risking small wars. Indeed, he thrives on crisis. But he remains a symbol of festering discontent. We cannot afford to appear in opposition to this comprehensible force. We must resist his efforts to make off with other lands by plotting. But we should not deny his legitimate aspirations.

It was foolish for the United States to sponsor military intervention in Lebanon without specific U.N. authorization. Such intervention had no sensible strategic objective comparable even to the ill-fated Suez adventure. At least that aimed at an international waterway. This is not to say we ought to have sat back and permitted Nasser to gobble up another satrapy. But there are conventional rules under which we can work. We could have insisted on expanding United Nations operations and pressed for the compromise that later worked out with Chehab as president.

Chehab's predecessor, Camille Chamoun, was a staunch friend of the West. He refused to break relations with London and Paris during the Suez war. He was the only Arab boss to accept the flabby Eisenhower Doctrine. But that doctrine could not save him. It specifies our aid only against threats by "international communism." Most of Nasser's Communists are in jail.

It is certainly in our interest to advertise that America's

friends can rely on America. But it seems silly to choose a confused issue. If Lebanon goes neutralist, as seems likely, we
might lose control of the remaining Middle East oil ports, and
these ports already depend on pipelines running through Nasser territory.

To Secretary Dulles's mind, trained as it is, the Anglo-
American expedition to Jordan and Lebanon in no way appeared as "intervention" or "foreign domination." And technically it certainly was not. But to Nasser and the Arab crowds
who venerate him, such distinctions have no meaning.

Nasser regards his Syrian-Egyptian federation as the traditional "defensive line against outside aggression" that has applied since the days of Saladin. He considers the Baghdad Pact
or any other military link between an Arab state and external
powers as "a new sort of colonialism. We simply will not
accept any foreign domination," he said to me, pretending to
speak for all Arabs. "You Americans have neglected an understanding of the characteristics of the area. There must be solidarity between Arab countries. All Arab countries must stand
back of each other. They must face danger from anywhere."

We, of course, disapprove of his methods. But we fail to
recognize that these are indigenous to the region and accepted
by its peculiar standards: conspiracy, assassination, bribery
and gunmanship, distortion of the truth.

Nasser claims that he dislikes Communism's materialist
aspects. Nor does he fancy tying himself so closely to the Soviet
economy as is now the case. But these, to his adventurous
spirit, are relatively minor matters. Like so many earlier
statesmen, he hopes to use Russia for his own ambitions without succumbing to its pressures. This aspiration is already
being subjected to serious test.

If one looks back on our vertiginous Middle East diplomacy
since the summer of 1956—Aswan, Suez, Eisenhower Doctrine, Lebanon; war, brink of war, brink of summit—one cannot help being impressed by the marvelous acrobacy displayed.

But it is time to look for a sounder policy foundation than a tightrope.

What are our aims in the area? There is no reason why the United States should oppose the principle of Arab unity. Indeed, we supported the short-lived Iraq-Jordan federation; we would not object to an eventual link between Morocco, Tunisia, and Algeria; and we admitted the Syrian-Egyptian union when we recognized it.

It might be wise for us once again to make some mild show of approval for Nasser's new state in order to demonstrate that it need not look only to Russia for help and psychological sympathy. But we cannot go too far. We cannot abandon our friends elsewhere, now openly reviled by Cairo.

What we must make plain is that, while we have no objection to Nasser's confederation or to its extension through peaceful, voluntary adherence by other lands, we cannot tolerate moves to expand it by conspiracy or force. This need not be said by public declaration. We have tended to make too many such statements in the past. They have a hollow ring.

It is now necessary that Washington revert wholly to conventional diplomacy and that it abjure proclamations. The latter do no good. They are willfully distorted by our enemies and often embarrass our friends. Furthermore, we should consult continually with our allies on how to calm the threatening situation in this area. Such countries as West Germany, Italy, Greece, and even Pakistan have vital interests in preserving Middle Eastern peace and keeping the area free of Communism. They are in a position to help.

In dealing with Nasserism we must remember that we are dealing with a movement that is more psychological than ideological. It demands a special kind of attention and solace. We ourselves during our early republican years (as Nasser hastens to point out) aspired to similar consideration.

The most important thing right now is to try to assuage his

excitable propaganda. Nasser neither likes nor comprehends what the free world's press says about him. Angered, he orders his own publicity apparatus to call us "pythons." This, unfortunately, is normal language for Arab publicists and is regarded as satisfactory rebuttal to sober criticism. Cairo must be encouraged to pipe down.

We shall have to behave with restraint in assaying this unsteady area. There are a lot of fuses burning. It is up to us to try to cool the atmosphere. By expressing private sympathy for Nasser's expressed aims but not his employed methods, we need not abandon our shrinking coterie of friends. There is no point getting mixed up in the Arab world's family rows.

Levelheaded courtesy in pronouncing our opinions is requisite; that and firmness. These people crave recognition as serious equals, such as is implied by normal politeness. Nasser still bristles at the rude way Dulles withdrew our offer to help build his high dam. He did not mind the withdrawal so much as how it was done. And undoubtedly he particularly savored the revenge of accepting a substitute Soviet offer in 1958.

In discussing these matters with some of our eager representatives in the Levant, one frequently hears the sad remark: "It is time we really began to behave like a big power out here." What is meant is this: The United States must appear more self-confident, less excitable, impervious to sudden bursts of temper in those parts. Bland steadiness in explaining our fundamental views will gain us much more than irked press-conference statements or frenetic special missions.

Nobody is yet sure just what American Middle Eastern policy is. Too often it appears to be merely a wavering series of asseverations. While we make our minds up, it might be well to maintain a poker face.

Nasser has problems. Egypt's economy is faltering and Syria is not rich enough to bolster it. There is a limit to Soviet aid. Nasser would like to restore some balance to his situation between the great power blocs even if he all too recently talked

about Russia as if it were seventh heaven. Right now he is in a
condition of emotional crescendo, proclaimed a new Saladin by
his supporters. He is inexperienced in international affairs and
has scant inkling of what too close a friendship with Moscow
may imply. Perhaps some helpful ambassador might lend
him a copy of A. E. Housman's "Demise of an Imperceptive
Youth," which recounts:

> The grizzly bear is huge and wild;
> He has devoured the infant child.
> The infant child is not aware
> It has been eaten by the bear.

In the Middle East we cannot, as Wilson did in Europe,
search for magicians and princesses in a world of dreams. Wilson's Secretary of State, Robert Lansing, practiced a "let the
dust settle" policy toward Russia after the Bolshevik revolution.
Acheson sought to do the same for Truman in China. It might
be well for our present administration to let the dust settle in
the Middle East—and keep Moscow from stirring up the eddies.

Whether this can work remains to be seen. The area is so
inspirited with racial, religious, economic, political, and social
frenzy that it is hard to imagine establishment of even relative
calm. Almost every nation in the Levant is intent on blackmail. In the background is a tradition of assassination and military coups. Ever since the Zionist Stern Gang murdered Lord
Moyne in Cairo during World War II, bullets have been accepted in the Middle East as a convenient means of expressing
political opinion.

In any case, we should remember that there are, in diplomacy, four cardinal rules: (1) always keep the initiative,
(2) always exploit the inevitable, (3) always keep in with the
outs, (4) never stand between a dog and a lamppost. Where,
in the past, we went wrong was in ignoring these precepts. We
have now seen the folly of violating rules one and four—

above all, vis-à-vis Cairo. Henceforth we must concentrate on rules two and three.

Initiative is not alone sufficient to gain our objectives. Nor is it enough merely to extricate ourselves from a position where small enemies and big friends could ignore us with insulting impunity. If we are eventually to create a tidy pattern out of chaos in the Levant, we must see clearly what trends are inevitable in that region. If we do not exploit them, Nasser or the Russians will.

One such trend is the increasingly intense search for popular government. Apart from Lebanon, standards of literacy and living are startlingly low within the Arab world. Yet, thanks to radio and films, it has been projected with dizzy speed into the modern political era. Uneducated *fellahin* are now very much aware of the insufficient benefits they receive from prevailing governmental systems.

This favors the activities of "outs," the opposition. And there is opposition everywhere. We saw it explode in Jordan, Lebanon, and Iraq. It even exists in Saudi Arabia, where members of the royal family were involved in a Nasser-inspired plot against the King. It is as necessary for us to be in contact with non-Communist "outs" in those countries as it is, for example, useful to retain intimate connections with British Labor leaders and German Social Democrats—something we have not always done.

This is far from easy. Ours is not a conspiratorial system, like that of the Soviet Union. We do not wish or intend to practice subversion to accomplish our objectives. Nor are these objectives as simple to define as those of Moscow: world revolution and Communist domination.

Nevertheless, in the social field we must press for greater distribution of wealth. Too many oil royalties benefit only royalty. Iraq and Kuwait alone among the Arab lands tried to show how such funds can benefit a populace.

In the psychological field we must encourage moderate elements to regain control of educational and propaganda facilities from Moscow and Nasser, for so long its cold-war cobelligerent. Here we and our friends are starting late. Even in friendly Kuwait and Libya, the proportion of Egyptian-trained teachers is immense. And what most of them teach is anathema to us.

Our difficulty, in the long run, is that we have no absolute idea to peddle, unlike Soviet Russia with its Big Lie technique. We can demonstrate at least that we are prepared to stand up firmly for the half-truth.

The goal of our Middle East diplomacy should not be merely to restore the *status quo,* either geographically or politically. In reality, there was no recognizable *status quo.* That is the root of the trouble.

Three changes must be reckoned with in any effort to stabilize the Levant: the rise of Arab nationalism, the weakening of the Western position, and the coincidental strengthening of Soviet influence. But history does not require that change bring chaos. To avoid such chaos the region must be sealed off from Great Power clashes. Neither bloc at present can hold the area and each wishes to deny it to the other. Likewise, a curb on local aggression, both direct and indirect, must be created. And finally, Western Europe's access to Arab oil must be protected.

In approaching these objectives we should take special pains to maintain our alliance ties, above all to Britain, France, and NATO. But that does not mean we are obliged to endorse each national aspiration of every ally.

Two salient facts must be faced. The first is that henceforth Russia's right to a voice in Middle Eastern affairs has to be acknowledged. The second is that we cannot escape certain special obligations to nations impinging on the Arab world. For example, as that region is neutralized, Turkey, Iran, and Israel become eligible for additional security guarantees from us.

Within this framework it does not seem impossible to rec-

oncile our views with Moscow's stated aim of guaranteeing the Middle East from external interference and freezing
arms shipments to the area. We must first define the territory
affected. Then we must insist on excepting from this embargo
countries with particular responsibilities, such as Turkey.

It is immensely difficult to try to insure the Levant against
indirect aggression, today a greater danger than that of direct
attack. One text to work from was once drafted by Molotov.
In 1939, when Moscow, London, and Paris sought unsuccess-
fully to negotiate an alliance against Germany, the Soviet Foreign Minister proposed that the three nations agree to help
each other in the event of Nazi aggression—"direct or indirect"—against any European state. In a special annex Molotov
suggested this obligation should apply in case of "internal
coup d'état or a political change favorable to the aggressor."

It is not beyond possibility for the U.N. to devise similar
machinery to thwart subversion by expansionists. If we can
come to an essential agreement on neutralizing the Middle
East, surely some mechanism can be invented to protect that
area from its own internal combustion.

The question of oil is vital to Britain and the Continent,
which depend for their existence upon access to this Arab
commodity. Might we not be well advised to let London and
Paris take the lead in negotiating settlement of this issue? We
would lose little by retiring from that prominent position we
have attained in Middle Eastern matters. About all this has
gained us is the role once held by the aggressors of Suez as the
favorite Arab whipping boy.

We should, of course, assist our friends in strengthening
their position as they begin to bargain. We must help them to
store larger petroleum reserves and to develop their nuclear-
power programs such as Euratom, thus making them less subject to potential blackmail pressures.

But beyond this we need not go. All of us must recognize
the existence as a major force today of the nationalism sym-

bolized by Nasser. Our aim should be to cease pressing this into Russia's arms; to prevent the U.S.S.R. from attaining dominance in the Middle East; and to protect the legitimate access of our allies to its petroleum. This provides foundation for a logical policy. And such a policy would be consonant with our long-term interests.

In the Middle East we should stop sponsoring crash programs, mere reactions to events. It is high time we set about defining the peculiar regional attributes of the area and adjusting our national interests to these special features. The first thing to recognize is that there are no natural frontiers and few stable countries there. We cannot agree with Moscow on some form of international armistice lines, as in other East-West deals over Berlin, Austria, Trieste, Korea, and Vietnam.

South of Turkey and Iran, excepting Israel, lies what we call the Arab world. Its people are bound by common Semitic race, the same approximate language, and similar religion, although this is divided by sectarianism. The so-called countries in which they dwell are relatively new creations. The wealth of this region is oil. And the only natural market for that oil in the foreseeable future lies in Western Europe. Neither Russia nor the United States can usefully absorb it.

Roughly speaking, the Middle East forms a peninsula joining two continents, Eurasia and Africa, thus enjoying particular strategic importance. The peninsula's base lies in the U.S.S.R., whose southern republics in the Caucasus and central Asia include millions of people who might almost be called Middle Eastern. Near its southern apex is one of the globe's most important canals.

Thus, there is an interesting superficial resemblance to the position of Central America. The base of the Central American peninsula lies among the Catholic Spanish-speaking ethnic groups of our own Southwest. It joins two great continents, and a canal bisects it. We have always been vitally interested in

Central America. Indeed, when a regime sympathetic to our opponents was installed in Guatemala, we ousted it.

Likewise, although hitherto without real voice, Russia has eyed the Middle East avidly. In 1940, during the era of Moscow-Berlin co-operation, Molotov memorialized Hitler demanding: "The area south of Batum and Baku in the general direction of the Persian Gulf should be recognized as the center of the aspirations of the Soviet Union."

For decades British policy sought successfully to keep the Russians from achieving such aspirations. We inherited this policy when Britain weakened after World War II. But the disagreeable fact is that the U.S.S.R.'s influence has now been extended diplomatically, economically, and, through arms deals, militarily into the Arab world. After three years of self-deception, we must admit this.

This does not mean we need abandon it to Soviet hegemony. Nasser emphatically agrees with us on that. Nevertheless, it does mean we can no longer pretend to exclusive influence of our coalition in the Middle East. Thus, one of our aims should ultimately be to keep the important region concerned from belonging to either power bloc. This is a political necessity.

Economically, we must insure that its oil continues to flow toward Western Europe, the only rational market. And we must avoid the appearance of seeking to freeze the existing governing situation. We sponsor the remaining Northern Tier governments, after the Iraqi coup. Does that mean we now undertake to insure present administrations in Iran and Pakistan, both Baghdad Pact members? Supposing there is a move, stemming from popular discontent, to upset either Teheran's Shah or the dictator in Karachi, and supposing this receives external encouragement from, shall we say, Nasser or Nehru, do we automatically and militarily oppose it?

This is a weighty consideration. We must remember that not many Asian governments are widely liked. There is uneasiness in both Iran and Pakistan. By our combined Baghdad

Pact and anti-indirect aggression pledges, do we guarantee their present systems? Our own proclaimed objectives encourage change in a considerable portion of the world, for example, Hungary and China. Should we not, therefore, ponder the practical application of our evolving theories? We do not seek aggression of any sort. But it requires uncanny precision to outlaw its indirect form without risk of freezing the political *status quo*.

And, finally, no policy for the Middle East can dodge the unfortunate consequences of Palestine's partition. There are two successor states to the old mandate, Jordan and Israel. Jordan cannot continue indefinitely in its current form. It lives on charity alone, an international remittance man.

Furthermore, in assaying the regional situation, an incalculable factor is the desperate hardiness of the new Israeli nation. It was hammered on a terrible anvil. Plenty of young women's arms still bear the tattooed numbers of Nazi prison camps. Officials observe calmly: "I have no relatives. Hitler took care of that."

Israel's people are not reluctant to take risks in their own defense. And David Ben-Gurion, the country's grand old man, is renowned for his tough-mindedness. It is unlikely he will ever accept Arab military preponderance over Israel—without attempting to forestall it.

The truculence and mutual suspicion of the Israelis and the Arabs is continually heightened by the awful problem of the million Palestine Arab refugees. Essential to any area settlement are solution of this tragic question and that of sharing limited supplies of water. Iraq has a real need for population. Surely it offers a better future for the unhappy Palestine Arabs who, at present, have nothing to lose but their misery. The U.N. should contribute for such relocation and ask Israel to pay suitable compensation.

Only in terms of such an arrangement can the all-important business of water-sharing be realistically approached. But none of the Arab states will sign a peace with Israel. And not until such a peace comes will economic logic replace nationalistic passions. Someday among the Great Powers there must be a re-examination of the Palestine problem. In that hitherto insoluble question are joined virtually all emotional threads of the explosive Middle East.

Arab nationalism receives unifying impulses from enmity toward Israel. Petroleum disputes impinge both on that country's Haifa refinery and its pipeline route from the Red Sea to the Mediterranean via Elath. And the cold war between the Western and Communist blocs is continually affected by a nervous Palestinian border where the U.N.'s only armed force is stationed.

It has proved impossible to devise a formula acceptable to both Arabs and Israelis. This is not a mere matter of adjusting frontiers and resettling refugees. The issue lies deeper. Most Arab leaders do not even dare admit Israel's right to exist. They fear assassination by fanatics. The prevailing theory of the latter is that some day there will be a final forceful reckoning when every Jew in Israel is driven into the sea.

On the other hand, an influential Israeli minority considers the present territory of that dynamic little state inadequate. This group would like to expand, taking over western Jordan, a bit of Syria, and the Gaza strip, now controlled by Egypt. A handful of ultras would go even further.

In 1958, during a long conversation in Cairo, Nasser complained: "Every day I am waiting for news of another invasion. This is the condition today—fear, no trust and no confidence. Tomorrow I am waiting for invasion."

I inquired: "You mean that as long as Israel exists there is a danger?"

"Yes," he said. "That is what we feel. That is the lesson of history."

And the Israelis are even more afraid, as indicated by Ben-Gurion's appeal for Soviet mediation that same year.

Between these extremes the framework of compromise must be devised. And it must be devised by the Great Powers. They have to discover a solution and impose it, for it was they who created, aided, and recognized Israel.

Since 1950 the United States, Britain, and France have jointly claimed responsibility for preventing forcible change of the Palestine borders—a responsibility violated in the Suez war. Russia, excluded from this pledge, has been free to imply support of every Arab complaint. This gives Moscow a notable propaganda asset in Islam. But any contemplated Palestine peace must be arranged in association with the U.S.S.R., if, as is evident, it must be externally imposed. Have not certain events since the 1958 Iraqi coup rendered this more feasible?

When we talked of a summit meeting to discuss Middle Eastern affairs with Khrushchev, we inferentially admitted his right to a say in that area's affairs. And the Levant's role in the global conflict has become different. There is today a greater interest in neutralizing the region, as between power blocs, and throttling its supply of outside arms.

Finally, with the new character of the Baghdad Pact, our relationships with Nasser may eventually alter. There is no longer any Arab aspect to that alliance without Iraqi partnership. Instead, it has become a means for us to give special guarantees to non-Arab Turkey and Iran before discussing neutralization of all Arabia.

In any future negotiations, can we ask Moscow to share in responsibility for Palestine? Certainly this would complicate the hitherto easy propaganda role we have left to the Russians. But is Khrushchev realistic enough to see the inevitability of further explosions, with their implicit global risk, if the imbalance of an armed Middle East continues?

Does he recognize that the existing situation cannot endure without another explosion? If, for example, Nasserism engulfs Jordan (as it has sworn to do), Israel will attempt to occupy that land's western half. Then at least a little war is inevitable. And Khrushchev dislikes the thought of conflict spreading near his southern limits.

Even Nasser admits by inference that the only Palestine solution must be composed if not imposed by outside powers. He said to me: "This is not something that can be simply decided on paper; that Israel must be liquidated; or that Israel must stay. We are not the only power to decide that."

Obviously, there is no question of Israel's liquidation. Therefore, the powers to decide how it must survive are, in fact, those Great Powers, including Russia, who helped create that courageous little nation. Even Soviet strategy does not appear to contemplate world conflict on the battlefield. Soviet strategy, to reword Clausewitz, is to regard peaceful policy as a continuation of war by other means. But it has sought to avoid the kind of international holocaust that another Middle Eastern flare-up might produce.

Chapter 7

The Logic of the Bursting Chinese Shell

Each passing year the Far East assumes increasing importance to the United States. During the first half of this century, despite the rise of a highly industrialized Japan, it was Europe that held by far the greatest specific gravity in terms of power external to ourselves. But this situation is changing. Europe, despite its genius for administration, its astonishingly high level of culture and thought, its concentrations of factories and transportation systems, must inevitably decline on the scale of global influence.

The reverse is true in the Orient, where more than half of the people now living dwell. For decades the equipment that will someday give this population an effective voice has been pouring eastward. Japan is already a brilliantly competent manufacturing power. Soviet Asia will soon be more important in shaping Moscow's opinions than Soviet Europe. India, slowly but inevitably, is being modernized. And China, the incredibly enormous state of mainland China, will almost surely be the greatest superstate existent when the twenty-first century rolls around.

It is, therefore, primarily in terms of China that one must assay our foreign policy as expressed in the Far East. And one might observe that, during recent years, we have shown al-

193

most as much genius in extricating ourselves from crises involving that country as we have shown genius in getting into such crises unnecessarily.

It is curious how emotionally involved we have tended to become about the Chinese. They first were intimately introduced to us as peon labor in the nineteenth century when they hammered railway spikes, washed shirts, and were immortalized as clever heathens by the delightful Bret Harte.

Our traders, our businessmen, and our missionaries began to swarm across that vast land. As they came to know its excellent inhabitants and to respect their magnificent heritage, they developed sentimental attachments. These still befog efforts to achieve a realistic approach to the China problem.

Franklin Roosevelt had a vision of the future when he insisted, contrary to the advice of his allies, that China be admitted prematurely to Great Power status and granted a permanent seat in the U.N. Security Council. But when, by immutable forces, unforeseen in Washington, revolution overthrew the government desired by Roosevelt as his Asiatic friend, we were acutely embarrassed by the international role we had devised for China.

Since that moment we have wandered lonely in a cloud of self-deception and wishful thinking. Contrary to our own diplomatic traditions and to all good sense, we have refused to recognize the Peiping regime. Yet recognition should have nothing whatsoever to do with approval or disapproval.

We imposed an embargo and an economic blockade to which our allies, for the most part, adhered, in order to hasten the end of a regime we disliked. The only consequence of this was to force the Chinese more closely into Moscow's arms. If ever there was a chance (which is debatable) of prying apart the two Communist giants, we did our best to avoid it.

Our policy encouraged China's rapid industrialization with Soviet aid and the mobilizing of its human forces. It assured that its educational program, now turning out more teachers, doctors, and engineers each year than the United States, would be violently slanted against us.

In dealing with China, we did not remember that diplomatic recognition should not be used as a weapon. Indeed, there is much to say for a policy of maintaining even more extensive relationships with your enemies than with your friends. We should always be in a position to ascertain, through our own trained observers, what such enemies are up to. (Although, in this case, during the McCarthyist era, we managed to purge from our Foreign Service the most able observers we might have sent.) This is above all true with respect to a tightly closed society.

England and France are open books where we can know what is taking place with or without embassies. China is a shut book. Yet we have refused to even peer into its critically important pages. We kept out our diplomats and banned our press. This is insanity.

We made of the China recognition issue a totally unnecessary issue. Now it has become acutely difficult to resolve because it involves our whole prestige. Yet what are the facts of diplomatic custom, including our own? It is a fundamental rule of international law that every independent state is entitled to be represented internationally by a government habitually obeyed by the bulk of the state's population, and which also exercises effective authority within its territory. During the past century there are few instances of irrevocable refusal of recognition on the sole ground that the government in question originated in a revolution. American relationships with such countries as the Soviet Union, Yugoslavia, Cuba, and Spain have all eventually been traced according to normal custom.

United States policy on recognition was perhaps first set when President Washington, by receiving Citizen Genêt in 1793, recognized the new revolutionary government of France. Much later, in 1822, the House of Representatives Committee on Foreign Affairs declared: "Who is the rightful sovereign of a country is not an inquiry permitted to foreign nations, to whom it is competent only to treat with the 'powers that be.' "

In 1856 President Franklin Pierce said: "It is the established policy of the United States to recognize all Governments without question of their source or their organization or of the means by which the governing persons attain their power, provided there be a Government *de facto* accepted by the people of the country."

This is a policy in most countries that regard recognition as in no sense signifying political approval or disapproval. Thus, Karachi recognized Communist China although Pakistan is an anti-Communist state. But American attitudes departed from traditional approaches under Woodrow Wilson, and have wavered ever since. Wilson, disapproving of Victoriano Huerta in Mexico, said he would not recognize governments founded by violent acts.

Herbert Hoover's Secretary of State, Henry L. Stimson, modified this to deny recognition to governments apparently imposed forcibly by foreign powers. Cordell Hull favored withholding recognition from regimes seizing power unconstitutionally until it was certain they were "in possession of the machinery of the state," had ended substantial popular resistance, and were in a position to fulfill international obligations. However, in 1948 the Truman administration reaffirmed the view that "the establishment or maintenance of diplomatic relations with a government does not imply an opinion on the domestic policy of that government."

We managed to befuddle ourselves whenever we injected politics or ideology into the recognition issue. This, which applied to the U.S.S.R. until 1933, still applies in the instance of the Vatican. It is nonsensical that we do not exchange ambassadors with the Holy See, as do so many other non-Catholic nations. The Vatican, quite apart from its religious significance, has great political importance as a lay state through its able and extensive foreign service. But, because we fear the objections of disgruntled American voters, we have refused to enter into normal diplomatic relations.

There is similar illogic with regard to Communist China. In this particular instance, furthermore, we have mixed with the recognition question that of admitting disliked governments to international bodies. We have refused this privilege to Communist China, and, thanks to our great influence, have made it stick. But what is the point? Why, for example, ban from the U.N. a country that presents the U.N. with one of its basic problems? We cannot even apply the moral influence of being in a position to ask it to withdraw. Yet China's voice is nevertheless heard on this high public platform, for we give the delighted Russians a chance to serve as the only channel of Peiping's views.

Even Dulles was aware of this paradox before he became secretary of state. Indeed, in 1950 he held what many of his opponents would now term realistic opinions on China. And, despite deeply indignant emotions stirred by the Korean war, he reaffirmed these in 1957. They were expressed in both the earliest and latest editions of his book *War or Peace*.

The Secretary wrote: "All nations should be members [of the U.N.] without attempting to appraise closely those which are 'good' and those which are 'bad.' Already that distinction is obliterated by the present membership of the United Nations. Some of the present member nations, and others that might become members, have governments that are not representative of the people. But, if in fact, they are 'governments'—that is, if they 'govern'—then they have a power which should be represented in any organization that purports to mirror world reality. If the Government of China in fact proves its ability to govern China without serious domestic resistance, then it, too, should be admitted to the United Nations. However, a regime that claims to have become the government of a country through civil war should not be recognized until it has been tested over a reasonable period of time."

In May 1952 Dulles met Eisenhower for the first time in Paris. Soon afterward, it became probable he would be chief diplomatic officer of an Eisenhower administration. Nevertheless, his previously published judgments worried some party stalwarts. Before the inauguration, Republican legislators representing the Know-Nothing faction inquired if Dulles still favored Peiping's entry into the U.N. They indicated he might have difficulty in obtaining confirmation as secretary unless he clarified his stand.

Dulles gave private assurances that he no longer backed such a concession to Red China. Furthermore, he promised to give favorable consideration to any candidate his questioners might recommend as assistant secretary in charge of Far Eastern affairs. The choice of Walter Robertson resulted.

Robertson had made no secret of his conviction that Mao Tse-tung was a passing phenomenon and Chiang Kai-shek remained China's 'real' symbol. Indeed, in 1957 the affable Assistant Secretary assured me at a Washington party: "Mao has no more real influence than the first taxi driver who goes by outside." To call such a statement meaningless is to flatter it.

We are slowly emerging from this dream world. The process is bound to be delicate, difficult, and embarrassing. Whether it can succeed, so late in the day, depends heavily upon the proven ingenuity of Dulles. However, in a tight corner, he is brilliantly agile. One may be distressed that he took so long to face unpleasant truths and that, ever since the 1958 Quemoy crisis, he has been pressed to do so in humiliating circumstances. But one should encourage his efforts at last to adjust policy to facts. The process must be arduous and gradual. Patience is therefore necessary.

It is evident that much hard thinking is now going on in the

United States concerning our unsuccessful China policy. The difference between the Truman and Eisenhower administrations in applying that policy has been by no means so great as is sometimes imagined. The Democrats initiated the idea of economic blockade to cripple Mao Tse-tung and abandoned the thought of major armed intervention during the latter days of the Chinese civil war. The Republicans continued to rely on the useless blockade. But at times they contemplated the idea of an active military adventure.

It would be foolish not to recognize that we have now got ourselves into a position from which we cannot suddenly extricate ourselves. For false reasons, too much of our prestige and honor has become involved. Misinterpretations of abrupt actions or the logic behind them would inevitably redound to our discredit. Unfortunately, this even involves such questions as diplomatic recognition and Peiping's admission to U.N. These have become subjects of intricate negotiations.

Now, thanks to our artificial posture, were we to make what appeared to be concessions to Mao, the loyalty of the governing regime in Formosa might switch. This could lead to the peaceful transfer of that island to China, contrary to our desires or our interests. We must never forget that Formosa is riddled with mainland agents; that Peiping has made numerous offers of accommodation to high-ranking Nationalists; that these nationalists, many of them with relatives across the strait, are desperately homesick and now see little chance of a victorious re-entry to the mainland; that Chiang's own son, one of Formosa's most powerful figures, once lived in Stalinist Moscow and married a Russian; that when Chiang dies there is bound to be a leadership crisis involving the fundamental dispute between the two million Nationalist *émigrés* and the eight million indigenous Formosans whom they rule and who have little interest in the Asian continent.

In approaching this situation, it is evident we wish two things: to keep Formosa itself, which we regard as of military importance, out of Peiping's hands; and to avoid war. It is by no means certain that Mao is equally eager to avoid war. Marshal Tito, for example, thinks the contrary. War could perhaps be supported, in these nuclear days, more easily by a nation of 600,000,000 than by either Russia or the United States, who would blow each other to bits. But there is reason to suspect Moscow joins us in our second aspiration on this China question, the preserving of peace.

Consequently, behind a smoke screen of stern statements, it has for long been apparent that we were trying to restrain our client in Formosa, and the Russians, it is indicated, sought to promote similar moderation in Peiping. The real bulls in the China shop are the Chinese themselves. Unfortunately, neither patron state, the U.S.A. or the U.S.S.R., can afford to appear too reasonable as far as the outer world is concerned, for, all too often, the outer world interprets reason as a sign of weakness.

Obviously, Washington does not want war. Equally obviously, Washington does not want to be dragged into war against its will. But our government is convinced that firm expression of ultimate intentions is required to avoid the drift toward such a war. We have, therefore, shown that, if there is no other way out, we will not shrink from conflict. This has been the essential meaning of American policy under two administrations during tempestuous moments in Greece, Berlin, Lebanon, and Formosa.

American public opinion became increasingly unhappy about Quemoy, a position hard to maintain either logically or logistically. But American public opinion will not accept bullying. It recognized, furthermore, that if the new imperialism is allowed forcefully to crumple existing barriers, vast areas behind those barriers might fall to our opponents. It is the very weakness of such areas that forced upon us a stubborn policy, after our original error in permitting ourselves to assume an essentially impossible stance.

To a large extent, this has been produced by past flaws in our diplomatic thinking. We ignored facts of history in the Middle East and Far East. And we paid for this lapse by awkward, makeshift decisions frightening to our friends and allies.

However, Moscow also cannot be too happy. When Khrushchev chopped down Stalin's reputation, he was, by inference, trying to trim the size of other Marxist giants, above all, Mao Tse-tung. He failed. Khrushchev apparently does not aspire to the Great Man myth himself. He is shrewd enough to perceive he cannot get away with it. But Mao has refused to yield either on Stalinism's methods or its hints of personal apotheosis. Despite his semiretirement, he continues to grow upon the Asiatic scene. His China now rivals Russia in the Orient. He intrudes in European matters. His interpretations of orthodoxy have been injected into purely Soviet disputes.

It suited Mao admirably to forestall a summit meeting in 1958 and explode another crisis with materials at hand in Quemoy. With his immense, unhappy population, he fears war less than others and reckons he has much to gain from threats. He can blackmail both his allies and his enemies before he agrees to stop.

Moscow may dislike the ugliness of such a situation. But it cannot afford to seem lukewarm in support of its only major ally. If Russia were to let down China, it would sacrifice incalculable prestige. And divisive forces latent within Communism might burst.

Likewise, we could never order Chiang Kai-shek abruptly to quit his remaining offshore toe holds simply to accommodate our NATO allies. Ultimately, this must happen, but not under pressure. We know Chiang would like to develop any conceivable emergency into a world war, his last, desperate gamble. This we do not intend to allow. But if we appeared to weaken in our support of his untenable posture, we feared losing esteem in Asia, and encouraging Formosan elements that might wish a deal with the Peiping regime.

Thus, neither Washington nor Moscow is any longer a completely free agent. Each is subjected to strong influences from client states who are prepared to be more bellicose than their patrons.

The tergiversations of our own China policy have been deeply influenced by a curious legacy of emotion. Wishful thinking has been allowed to replace in our minds this world's bleak realities. Such was true during World War II, during the ensuing civil conflict, and during the later period of two Chinas.

The desire to make a great power from the massive Kuomintang chaos was a noble dream. It was compounded of hope, illogic, anti-Japanese feeling, and failure to appreciate either the forces behind Mao Tse-tung or Moscow's ultimate hopes. Even Churchill remonstrated during the 1943 Cairo conference that our objective would be impossible to realize. Nevertheless, the deep affection entertained by generations of Americans for the admirable Chinese people helped inspire political determination to achieve the unachievable. With one eye blind to Chiang's weakness and the other eye blind to Mao's strength, we persevered. To our later embarrassment we insisted China be admitted as one of five permanent nations on the Security Council.

As early as 1948, Dulles, then Republican adviser to the State Department, saw the difficulties ahead. He predicted that if Chiang fled to Formosa the Security Council would be permanently weakened when other governments acknowledged a mainland Communist regime. This has, of course, happened. When Dulles negotiated the Japanese peace treaty for Acheson, he sought a formula whereby both Communist and Nationalist China could sign—without prejudicing either's status in terms of international recognition.

Influence of a well-financed Kuomintang lobby, search for dramatic issues in our own intraparty political debate, and feelings of deceived helplessness joined to strengthen United

States determination to stick by Chiang. For years we pretended to ourselves that he would be able to return to the mainland—even after Mao managed a successful amphibious operation against well-garrisoned Hainan. When the Korean war broke out, our military planners decided Formosa was too valuable a base to permit in Communist hands. Both Mao and Stalin coveted the island which could outflank Japan and the Philippines.

Having made a basic strategic decision, thus reinforcing our sentimental and political approaches, we found ourselves committed to back Chiang or his successors. We dodged consideration that longer-range policy must ultimately imagine a permanent destiny for the island and its nonmainland majority of Formosans. We continued to withhold recognition from Peiping and pressed our friends to do likewise.

This paid off in disgruntlement. Despite our arguments, Britain, members of its Commonwealth, and many Western nations opened embassies in Peiping. We obtained their agreement to limit trade with Mao. But the structure of commercial limitations eventually leaked to our own disadvantage. Our allies, economically pressed, resented attempts to curb their search for Eastern markets. Dulles himself—before he became secretary—foresaw that Japan and Southeast Asia would suffer if we barred them from normal China trade.

Inevitably, history made it necessary for us to start slowly modifying our unrealistic attitude. Yet, curiously enough, Moscow gave simultaneous hints of a readiness to ignore certain of Peiping's ambitions. The Russians sought to obtain a formula for limiting atomic weapons to the three powers first possessing them—the United States, the U.S.S.R., and Britain. What this meant was that Washington and London would guarantee that neither France nor West Germany could have such armament if Communist China were excluded. (France now virtually has its A-bomb.)

The Kremlin stood to gain in two ways. On the one hand,

the nuclear club would be deprived of two Western members. France already had an incipient atomic-arms program. And Moscow fears Germany. On the other hand, the Chinese behemoth on Russia's eastern flank would be kept in permanent military inferiority. We do not need Franco-German nuclear production. But we apprehend a Communist China armed with atom bombs. Russia, however, seems to have similar anxieties, for Moscow not only endeavored to exclude Peiping from nuclear-weapons manufacture, but refused its client state these and similarly modern arms when the request was made.

One of our problems in analyzing the Chinese situation has been that of China's sons and daughters who live abroad. The greatest potential fifth column in all Southeast Asia is the so-called overseas Chinese population of some twelve million industrious people dwelling in that polyglot multinational area. Yet, United States foreign policy, so clearly aware of this group's latent threat to regional stability, seems intent upon maximizing rather than minimizing its ultimately dangerous possibilities. We appear to take little interest in encouraging assimilation of the Chinese-speaking minorities (in Singapore, a majority) within that restless portion of the world. Instead, we focus propaganda efforts upon popularizing among them the Formosan government of Chiang Kai-shek. This we imagine to be a magnetic attraction capable of offsetting Peiping's increasing pull.

Such is shortsighted, dead-end thinking. To begin with, the overseas Chinese are not a uniform mass with a single heritage and tradition. They derive from all over China, speak different dialects, have various customs. But scarcely any originated in Chiang's present dwindled domain. Consequently, although many are strongly anti-Communist, they are bound to Formosa by no passionate devotion. Time has dimmed hopes of any Nationalist return to China. And some of the more acute *émigrés* realize that Formosa's future belongs not to those who inherit Chiang's mainland claims but to the Formosan people—a majority of that strategically located island. With those Formosans the overseas Chinese have no link.

Nevertheless, our government seeks to galvanize interest only in Chiang. This is a fallacious approach. If it made sense some years ago, when there still was talk of "liberating" China, it makes nonsense now. It would be wiser were Washington, both through normal diplomatic activity and through propaganda, to encourage overseas Chinese to take part as normal citizens in the communities where they reside—as in the United States.

A helpful role can be played in Southeast Asia by these hard-working, intelligent people, so many of whom have no taste for Marxism. But it will not be easy to foster such assimilation. In the Philippines there is prejudice against the Chinese, who have gained a firm commercial foothold. Newly independent Malaya fears a Chinese ethnic majority should Singapore ever unite with that fledgling state.

What is the alternative to equality and firmer local ties? If the Chinese are cold-shouldered in lands like Burma, Thailand, and Indonesia, they are bound to hanker only after the two available poles—Peiping and Taipei. But the electricity is running swiftly out of Taipei.

The threat implicit in this awkward situation is plain. In 1955 Jakarta police confiscated a batch of textbooks being distributed among Chinese-speaking residents. These displayed maps showing China as including all the Southeast Asian mainland plus much of Indonesia. Overseas Chinese were being taught that someday Peiping would sweep down and embrace them.

The "Chinatowns" of that area are quite distinctive from neighboring settlements. In Singapore, little old women, their pigtails twisted into buns, hurry along in their pajamas, shielding themselves with parasols from a burning sun. Quaint shops sell palm fans like motley banners. More than four-fifths of Singapore's inhabitants are Chinese. But Lim Yew Hock, first elected chief minister of that self-governing British colony and himself of Chinese extraction, has shown what the alternative to a "China" future is. He speaks three of his ancestral dialects but remains inherently English in culture and ideology.

Lim has fought for independence, and someday hopes for Singapore's union with Malaya. However, he opposes Mao Tsetung's efforts at subversion. He has quelled Communist-inspired riots, closed down suspicious schools, suspended incendiary publications, and deported fellow travelers. He is determined to demonstrate that his city's future is as an appanage of neither London nor Peiping.

This is a sensible course. Rather than oppose it, even by inference, we should encourage it. Because Chiang now means little to overseas Chinese, it is a hopelessly long odds gamble to build him as a symbol for their future. And were he to surprise the world by reconquering China, he, too, would probably assert imperial claims in Southeast Asia.

The overseas Chinese should take their rightful part in the lands where they have settled—not as a mere advance guard of distant empire. This is so evident that it is difficult to comprehend why our State Department has refused to acknowledge the realities. It will take years of patient diplomatic suasion to encourage more trust in these Chinese communities by their hosts. And years of propaganda among the emigrants is required to convince them where their true future lies. But it will take even longer if we do not start soon by recognizing facts. There is no place for oriental *Volksdeutsche*—to be exploited by some Asian Hitler.

Ever since he was driven from the continent, Chiang Kaishek has based his policy on the dream of someday returning. At times he hoped he could induce the United States to sponsor an armed invasion. But after the 1958 Quemoy crisis the best he could aspire to was a Hungarian-type mainland revolt

in which he could interfere. And for years it has been evident
—outside Taipei and Washington—that such aspirations were
but wishful thinking.

Twenty-five centuries ago that remarkable Chinese strat-
egist Sun Tzu wrote: "Supreme excellence consists in breaking the enemy's resistance without fighting." This has now
become Mao Tse-tung's objective when he looks across the
Strait of Formosa at his oldest enemy, Chiang.

Peiping gradually changed its tactics. While maintaining
powerful bases and armies on the opposite shore, it tends,
with flamboyant exceptions, to subordinate hostile military
gestures to undermining propaganda efforts. The Communists
created a "Work Committee on the Peaceful Liberation of
Formosa" headed by two former officials of Chiang's Kuomintang: General Chang Chih-chung and Dr. Wong Wen-hao,
once premier of the Nanking government. Relatives of distinguished Nationalists, summoned to Peiping Radio, invite the
émigrés home. Agents are infiltrated when possible. Chiang's
Chief of Staff, an able officer who had graduated from
both Virginia Military Institute and Purdue, had to resign in
embarrassment when it was disclosed that his aide was working for the Communists.

Clearly, Mao calculates time is on his side. Various problems in Formosa are coming to a head. Political leaders are
aging. Chiang himself is over seventy. Relatively few junior
or intermediate officials fled with him. The Formosans, subjects of Japan for fifty years, have no tradition of governing
experience. The next decade is bound to produce a leadership crisis.

Economically, the future is uncertain. With our approval,
Chiang maintains a disproportionately powerful armed force.
This cannot exist without massive American aid. Three-
fourths of Formosa's income goes to defense. The island's
gross national product must be increased 5 per cent annually
to keep economically afloat. That requires large capital in-

vestment. Chiang's, however, is, in effect, a one-party, semi-Socialist regime. Most key industries, such as aluminum, sugar, and power, are state-owned. Private investors are, therefore, not attracted. And our own government is under political pressure to reduce foreign aid. Furthermore, in theory, Washington favors free enterprise abroad.

Finally, there is the matter of morale. During a decade, confidence has been maintained by slogans promising return to the mainland. Their effect wore thin and now has virtually vanished. More and more Formosans are being recruited into the army. They are less interested than the emigrants in reconquering China.

Obviously, Chiang is aware of these factors. For this reason, presumably, he pressed us for a military decision. He insisted to me in several conversations that an attack on the mainland "would not lead to a general war," although he added somewhat contradictorily: "The only effective strategy against the Russian Communists' unlimited and protracted warfare is one of total war."

Chiang assured me in 1957: "If the democratic bloc should fail to make liberation its basic policy against Communism and Communist aggression, then all discussions about strategy and tactics are plainly futile." But is "liberation" American policy? Some years ago such indeed appeared to be the case. Washington proclaimed its faith in the mystic word—with all its belligerent implications. We boasted that Chiang had been "unleashed" against a crumbling Communist colossus. But now, in fact, the opposite is true.

If we preach "liberation," we practice "containment." Chiang has been leashed, not unleashed. In December 1954, we induced him to give a written guarantee not to attempt invasion except with our prior approval. He could hardly move a division across the strait without our help. And this was emphatically re-emphasized in the autumn of 1958.

The result is stalemate. In the long run, Mao calculates this will favor him. Washington somehow reckons otherwise. We believe that existence of this Nationalist army, plus Syngman Rhee's South Korean force achieves an East Asian power balance. Perhaps we hope Peiping's evident internal difficulties will someday produce a less rigid government with which we might be able to negotiate. Meanwhile, we do not want to relinquish any possible bargaining assets.

This complex statecraft is based more on faith than reason. Whatever we may think of Chiang's belligerence, there is at least logic in his desire to gamble on war. He has little to lose. But our own policy is containment masking as liberation. It is compounded of strategic interest and political emotion.

Formosa is an essential part of our Pacific fortress chain. And we have a guilty conscience toward Chiang. Once we saw him as our strongest Asian ally. Now we find him emperor of an Oriental Elba and imagine ourselves responsible. Yet we fear to let him risk his Waterloo. We are afraid to experiment with other ways of solving the impasse lest we might appear to be yielding. This produces paralysis. Chiang's logic is that of force, somewhat audacious in this nuclear era. Ours is founded on paradox; Mao's on time.

The confusion of the resulting impasse focused on the famous little offshore islands clustered about Quemoy and Matsu. For at least four years, the Communists have been strong enough to take these from Chiang unless the United States intervenes and if they are ready to accept heavy casualties. However, the tiny territories involved have little strategic importance. Therefore, we always wondered if we should gamble on such intervention and assume that it would not provoke Soviet reaction and World War III. We had to be certain that it was not in Moscow's interest to become militarily involved. And if we made a miscalculation, could we rest assured that our allies would support us in a conflict originating over Matsu and Quemoy? This decision has not yet been fully tested. Chiang won the 1958 artillery duel with

Mao, but when Peiping so wishes, it is obvious its 600,000,000 people can overwhelm the islands.

Washington had also to weigh the consequences of any formula that would hand over Matsu and Quemoy without a fight. Would we, as leader of the free world, be willing to abandon territories merely because they are faced with the threat of armed aggression?

The moral, psychological, and political aspects of this perplexing question were always of greater importance than its military significance. It was argued that the islands' loss would diminish support for Chiang Kai-shek's waning cause among the overseas Chinese population of Southeast Asia. It was contended that if we did not sustain Chiang in Matsu and Quemoy the morale of his forces would be shattered. And, finally, it was adduced that any decision to evacuate the coastal positions would be the equivalent of a "Far Eastern Munich."

Certainly there is evidence that the overseas Chinese long since abandoned Chiang. Those not influenced by Peiping's new grandeur seek their alternative in local affiliations, whether in Singapore or Manila—not Formosa. And while no doubt Nationalist spirits would be seriously dampened if Matsu and Quemoy were lost, unfortunately, there is no ultimate alternative for Chiang's followers. In the last analysis, they rely upon the support of the United States, not themselves.

The comparison with the betrayal of Czechoslovakia at Munich was never just. Can it be said that Chiang's cause would be substantially weakened if he were induced to give up positions that are economically valueless, militarily untenable, and juridically debatable? The Munich agreement turned over to Hitler the defenses of Czechoslovakia, rendering helpless the strongest country in Central Europe. And, as Bismarck foresaw and Hitler proved, the master of Bohemia is the master of Europe.

But the master of Matsu and Quemoy is not really master of anything. At a meeting of American ambassadors in 1955 at the Philippines resort of Baguio, the only two envoys with military experience, General J. Lawton Collins and Admiral Raymond A. Spruance, were asked to give views on the offshore islands. They both said the positions were strategically worthless. Their possession would not bring Mao Tse-tung materially nearer to the conquest of Formosa. Nor would their retention improve Chiang's chances of reinvading the mainland.

The two giants of the present moment, the United States and the U.S.S.R., are inextricably involved in the crisis between their Chinese protégés. Neither Washington nor Moscow can assuredly forecast the other's actions if extensive shooting starts upon the China coast.

Many of our military men, encouraged by Chiang, believed for a considerable time that an offshore-island battle would present us with an admirable chance to crush Mao's forces in a local war. But the use of tactical atomic weapons in such a conflict is not to be excluded. Would this not provoke Russian reaction? Could Moscow afford to stand by passively and watch the crippling of Peiping—even if willing to ignore the Sino-Soviet treaty? This seems unlikely. Effective American intervention in an offshore-island war seems calculated to bring Russian riposte. But we cannot count with similar assurance upon our own allies. Indeed, some of them have warned they will not support us in a conflict arising over Matsu and Quemoy.

Therefore, despite Formosa's victory in the 1958 Quemoy duel, it is necessary to find some formula that will erase the possibility of war over the islands. And this must go further than the existing informal arrangement. One idea broached has been that we should induce Chiang to abandon these positions if we can get assurances that the main democratic allies will join in opposing armed attack on Formosa itself. Another aspect being studied is the attitude of India. Many of our policy makers would like to attract the neutral powers of Asia into association with our barriers against aggression. If Chiang is ever persuaded by us to quit Matsu and Quemoy, would Nehru help offset the psychological shock in Asia by joining in the guarantee of Laos and Cambodia? Is India's attitude on the complex China question affected by ambitions to assume Chiang's Security Council seat? Oblique questions such as these must be explored. Meanwhile, the sands of time run out along the shores of China.

In the dialect of Fukien Province, looming stark across the way, the name of Quemoy means Golden Gate. Quemoy is a golden gate to nowhere. In between thunderous, meaningless, sudden battles, informal truce rules along China's only potential military front. On each side vast armies continue to modernize their equipment from Soviet and American arsenals. Peiping maintains no less than forty-four combat corps. Taipei keeps 587 generals and admirals on the active list and another 352 who are retired but subject to emergency recall.

Where are all these soldiers going? By signed agreement, Chiang has undertaken not to invade his homeland without Washington's approval. This is not forthcoming. We have sought also to induce Mao to renounce force. He has not openly done this. Yet he does not move in earnest. Has Moscow tacitly leashed him?

There is an aspect of unreality about such ponderous strength so delicately poised upon the brink of danger. Slowly the China crisis seems to be maturing from imminence of battle into what Trotsky once called "neither peace nor war." This is, of course, a source of savage disappointment to the aging Chiang. Each month of factual, if unadmitted, armistice sees a fading of his hopes to reconquer the mainland in his lifetime.

Really until 1958, in the atmosphere of political incest that for so long prevailed in Chiang's sadly shrunken domain, the belief reigned that the world revolved around Formosa. It was like the ancients' concept of the relationship of Earth to solar system. This egocentric view now must change.

There is awareness that a dramatic, sudden denouement is unlikely. The problem is now to persuade Taipei's tragic regime to build for a long term on the realistic, if unspoken, premise of two Chinas, still acceptable to neither Mao nor Chiang.

Chiang is becoming reconciled to the drear truths of a situation he can no longer pretend to control. His government is being persuaded to draw up durable programs for developing Formosa and its fragmentary island realm. Dreams of past glory are gradually merging into a more practical immediate future. This is, of course, galling to impatient, homesick *émigrés*. But it is a necessary and obvious response to two developments: the invention of nuclear weapons, which geometrically increases the danger of any war; and the assertion of American political control over Chiang's military strategy.

The Nationalist leader has, in effect, placed himself in bondage to the American people. Our public opinion must support him, and he is at last aware of this. Chiang knows we would never permit another "Hungary" in China. If Mao's subjects rise in rebellion, he hopes both he and we will join in aiding them. He knows we will safeguard his little island— in our interest and his own. But he also knows we will not let him lead us into battle.

Chiang cannot make war today, and we cannot make peace. Consequently, his nation of two million fugitives and eight million indigenous Formosans is being transformed by history from pretender to the mainland's destiny into an independent, separate island domain.

As long ago as 1955, Chiang protested to me, in his southern hideaway at Kaohsiung, about the pressure on him to abandon his offshore claims. At the time, he was resting and reading the works of two philosophers, Georg Wilhelm Friedrich Hegel and Wang Yang Ming. The writings of Hegel provided much of the background both for Hitler's Nazism and for Communist dialectics. Chiang explained that he was widening his acquaintance with the gloomy German in order to acquaint himself better with the basis of Communism. He believes in knowing his enemy. And he took comfort in Wang Yang Ming because that sixteenth-century scholar taught that true understanding must be combined with action; that for the man of wisdom it is not sufficient to know; he must act according to this knowledge. Chiang complained we would not permit such action, that already he was being asked to abandon the last, minute portions of mainland China not yet taken from him by the Communists, the tiny islands. He grumbled that ever since Yalta he had been deceived by allies; and now those same allies were demanding further sacrifices.

"It would not be fair," said he in soft tones but jutting out chin and lower lip, "to try to force us to give up the offshore positions without a fight. That would be contrary to all international justice and to the obligations of our allies. The United States should not accede to British ideas on this." The Generalissimo's voice rose and he gesticulated with his hands, saying: "Whether the United States joins in the defense of these islands or not they should not try to compel Free China, an ally, to give them up. Under no circumstances will our forces withdraw from them. We shall not yield to any pressure. We are determined to fight to the last man. And this may turn into the decisive battle for China."

Chiang was still talking of an imminent world war. He predicted that Moscow and Peiping would force a general conflict some time in 1956. He reasoned accordingly: Czarist Russia only tackled Japan, half a century ago, after the Trans-Siberian Railway had been completed. Rail links of equal strategic importance were then being constructed across Sinkiang and Mongolia to link the Soviet and Chinese systems. They would be ready in 1956. And then the Communist bloc would be spurred into all-out aggression by the pressure of internal economic and agricultural weaknesses.

To gain strategic freedom of action, our government has felt it necessary to align itself in the Far East with allies it previously avoided. We had carefully excluded Great Britain from the ANZUS agreements with Australia and New Zealand. We had hitherto kept quite apart from French military ties in Asia. When Senator William E. Jenner was talking vaguely about a PATO or Pacific Treaty Organization, Dulles opposed it. As recently as the Bermuda conference in November 1953, the Secretary of State argued that the United States had no intention of banding together with "the old colonial powers."

Dulles did not want to participate in any regional agreement that might lay us open to the charge of joining with imperialist countries. Instead, he hoped an Asian leader might emerge who could take the initiative in forming an alliance composed solely of free Asian nations and supported by us. But this dream never materialized.

Once we had joined SEATO, Dulles conceived of it strategically in terms of a hand with three fingers pointing toward Communist China. These fingers represented SEATO's own nominal armed strength, Chiang's forces in Formosa, and Syngman Rhee's in South Korea, all muscled to a palm represented by our own Pacific air and naval power. The Secretary of State envisioned all three fingers pressing together against Peiping if that capital threatened any one of them. But our other allies in the Southeast Asia pact, including Britain and France, would not agree. They refuse, for example, to commit themselves to helping Chiang from the SEATO area if he gets in an offshore-island war. Thus, the three-prong strategy is basically a delusion. We pay the piper; but we cannot call the strategic tune.

From our point of view, SEATO was perhaps a reluctant

alliance because of the formal link to colonial powers. But the only two Asian nations capable of taking the lead, India and Japan, were even more reluctant to take a stand in the same box with the colonial powers and to be bound, at least by Dulles's implication, to Chiang and Syngman Rhee.

Rhee is surely the world's most bellicose octogenarian, a man with the face of a benevolent Buddha, hair like thistle-down, and the heart of a jingo. Ruthlessly single-minded, he seeks only unification of a free Korea. With blatant frankness he admits this can be accomplished solely by war. Therefore, he wants war; and the sooner the better.

It is hard to associate this mild-mannered philosopher and his tastes for gardening, fishing, and the delicate calligraphy of China with the terrible goals he has set himself. "But," he once told me at his winter home in Chinhae, facing toward Japan across the water, "here in Asia we are on the frontier. We don't believe anyone can coexist with the Communists. They are advancing all the time. They improve their position daily. How long will you allow them to continue?"

The venerable President still gets highly excited as he talks. His inflections rise and he waves his hands. Mrs. Rhee, a cozy, plump Austrian lady, tried to calm him, serving cups of coffee and Viennese cake. "He comes here for a rest," she murmured. "He comes to work in the garden and to fish. Such fine fishing weather," she remarked, observing the great clouds lumbering outside like leaden whales.

But the President was off along the road to war. "I told General Eisenhower that the sooner we cripple Communist aggression, the better for the whole world," he said to me in 1955. "Eisenhower and Dulles can talk with the Communists all they want, but there is no other solution. Conferences lead only to disaster. You are saving the world for peace by yielding. That is no solution. You are avoiding war only by sur-rendering the world. You have to use force against gangsters trying to break into your house. You people are too afraid of war. If war is the worst thing you can imagine, then go ahead and surrender everything to avoid it. Give up your stocks of atom weapons. The only alternative to total surrender is war. And the sooner the better. Fewer lives will be sacrificed. Our allies are teetering too much." Rhee leaned back in his armchair, rumpling the sweater beneath his jacket and regarding, on the silk-covered table before him, the two volumes of ideographs he was reading at night to take his mind off this terrible world: Korean classics and a selection of Chinese Tang poems.

Mrs. Rhee pointed to a scroll hanging on the wall decorated with large calligraphic characters. "He wrote that for me on my last birthday," she boasted lovingly. "It is a poem, and in his own handwriting." The President turned around with a smile and translated. "A woman has three duties," he read. "A woman must be contented. And she must be pleased with simple living. And she must be happy doing her duty."

If the cold war lasts much longer, we may find it uneconomic to continue financing Rhee's massive South Korean army. Already, bound by armistice restrictions, we have had to clutter up our own production lines to keep manufacturing spare parts for his outmoded tanks, which cannot be replaced by new models. And we must not only maintain the South Korean army but support it with our mobile strength from distant island bases. Over any protracted period this will be impracticable, as Rhee himself takes pains to stress in somewhat hysterical terms.

Eventually, Korea will have to rely upon Japan for logistical support. Japan has considerable industry and already manufactures military transport, weapons, and ammunition. Where, Rhee wonders, will this leave Korea? He envisions the day when he will have to depend on his ancient adversary. And he refuses to accept such a position.

Rhee's country cannot exist indefinitely, above all, on a partitioned basis, unless the United States maintains its present rate of financial aid—which is unlikely. Yet we have pledged ourselves to rehabilitate South Korea, come what may. Our investment in blood, money, and promises is immense. It is hard to conjecture how we can make it pay off.

The final key is Japan. Our former enemy is now our only Asiatic friend with a powerful potential. Yet our military relationships with Japan are based on paradox. We imposed upon it a constitution forbidding all armed forces. By law the Japanese cannot fight even a defensive war. We also introduced democracy. This functions so well that a strong opposition prevents amendment of crippling constitutional limitations. The arrangement seemed all right in the peaceful world we dreamed of once. But it falters now.

After the Korean conflict started, we saw the illogic of the situation. At our behest, and quite illegally, the Japanese created an armed police and, from that nucleus, what was euphemistically termed a Self-Defense Force. This developed slowly—too slowly for our revised tastes. But the Japanese discovered advantages to living in an American-protected incubator. It is inexpensive. It insures democracy. When there is no army, or, at best, a weak one, there can be no revival of a dominant military class. And it is practical.

The Japanese know we must protect their islands in our own strategic interest. Therefore, they can invest industrial energy that might be expended on rearmament in the manufacture of export goods. As might be expected from all this, the result is distinct apathy on the subject of national defense. In 1954 we decided we could no longer afford to heavily garrison Japan, that, therefore, we must apply shock treatment to stimulate greater local effort. This took the form of notice that we intended to reduce and eventually to withdraw our forces.

But can Japan fill the vacuum now being created? The present answer is no. Tokyo is only obligated to aid us in repelling aggression against its own islands. No clause covers the possibility of another Korea or a Formosan war. Our present defense agreement allows us bases. But were we to try to operate from them in a conflict not resulting from attack on the Japanese, we might find the going difficult. A resentful population could sabotage our communications and render key points incommunicado. No matter what treaties say, we remain today as Tokyo's military guests. The weaker our presence becomes, the more this is true.

The paradox boils down to one all-important factor. Japan's ultimate defense shelters beneath the umbrella of our strategic striking power. In East Asian terms, where is that power based? Upon Okinawa—an island whose Japanese sovereignty we figuratively acknowledge. But our security treaty simply does not guarantee that Japan would fight beside us in any Pacific war. Therefore, our generals and admirals calculate we cannot relinquish Okinawa, a quintessentially important base. The threat of riposte from there is the greatest immediate deterrent to assault on the island chain extending through Japan and Formosa from the Aleutians to the Philippines.

This will remain the case for years to come, even when missiles replace planes. Our planners insist on retaining control of Okinawa as long as we face a powerful opponent in the Orient. Right now that seems to imply "forever." But our tenure of Okinawa increasingly poisons relations with Japan, America's most influential Eastern ally.

This embarrassment is still politely avoided in diplomatic exchanges. So, for that matter, is Article IX of the constitution forbidding Japan "the right of belligerence." We cannot afford to let the Japanese slip from our political sphere. But we are building forces which one day must repel it. "Paradox," says the dictionary, is a "seemingly absurd though perhaps really well-founded statement."

Almost eight centuries ago, a curious governing device originated in Japan: the *shogunate,* a kind of dictatorship coexisting with the throne. The *shogun,* or generalissimo, bore approximately the same relationship to the emperor as did Mussolini to the Italian king. From 1868 until 1945, there was no *shogun.* Not long after Commodore Matthew Perry's naval flotilla forced the Japanese to abandon self-imposed isolation, the Emperor Meiji did away with the traditional dictator. But fourteen years ago, in the wake of atomic war, a new *shogun* was installed in fact if not in name: General MacArthur.

Since the peace treaty, Japan has again been independent. Tokyo now has diplomatic relations with eighty other nations and a seat in the United Nations. But it still relies overpoweringly upon the United States. Uncle Sam continues to play the role of invisible *shogun* from Washington. American policy set the design for Japanese political development. Japan depends upon American trade. American diplomacy has erected a great wall between Communist China and Japan. American power remains the sole real military protection. This is based largely on Okinawa, which is Japanese in theory but American in control.

It is too much to expect that this is a happy foundation for enduring friendship. Do we deceive ourselves about our popularity? Is it human logic that a nation which relies upon us for existence should love us for that condition? Beneath the veneer of smiles is there disguised resentment? Do debtors like creditors?

We introduced an interesting replica of our democracy upon which the emperor is superimposed as a symbol. But few countries fit our particular pattern so little as does Japan. Our formula is devised for a rich, underpopulated land with enormous natural resources. Japan is small, overpopulated, and has no resources at all.

In effect, we teach the Japanese to live on an income they will never have. Even to approach the American way of life, their living space would have to multiply. Nevertheless, such is impossible unless Japan expands its territory. To avoid increase in the swollen population, 2,500 Japanese would have to emigrate each day. Where?

In Japan there has been a tendency to assume external habits of powers adjudged superior in strength. The United States, Germany, and England have all had periods of influence. The Japanese ape other civilizations in order to compete. But the nation's inner soul, so remote from foreign penetration, remains surprisingly unchanged. Our political philosophy was new and provoked great stimulus. But now there is vague groping for past forms. The Emperor, who emerged after 1945 as a popular constitutional monarch with only symbolic importance, is gradually retreating into remote mystery. One can only hope that the forthcoming marriage of the crown prince with a commoner will halt such a retrograde trend.

Nobody can pretend to foresee where these uncertain currents will lead. There is little likelihood of change while national prosperity continues—even if its level is far lower than ours. But a profound Japanese observer pointed out to me that his countrymen, throughout centuries, have had "long training in obedience." This enables them easily to accept radical metamorphoses such as that of the past decade. It could lead along other sudden paths.

A Tokyo professor believes: "Liberalism has neither done its work successfully nor taken deep root in this soil. Freedom in Japan is, even at the moment, in a precarious state. Should the tide begin to turn, the masses would move to the side of the totalitarians just as, we must confess, they did at the beginning of World War II. It would be impossible to win mass emotional understanding of the value of freedom so long as standards of living remain low. In order to stabilize society on the principle of freedom it is necessary to raise the living level. For this an enormous enlargement of the Japanese economy is necessary. It would be wrong to assume that liberalism is firmly implanted. Even among the higher classes it is only an abstract ideology. The poverty-stricken masses in the countryside were left entirely untouched by liberal ideas."

How can there be an "enormous enlargement" of the economy? Certainly there can be none so long as Japan is forced by circumstances to depend upon our benevolence. We are not going to buy much more than we already do. Therefore, the Japanese look to Asia for the future, above all, to China, from which we isolate them.

It is difficult for an American to understand the depth of this feeling. Japan remains an Asian country beneath the Western façade of its cities. China is Asia. We tell the Japanese there is really no commercial future with autarchic Peiping, that their dreams are only mirages. But even a mirage can induce thirst. Psychologically, man craves the forbidden. Here is the germ of a problem—what may someday be the quintessential problem of our *shogunate*'s legacy.

The Japanese have yet to recognize just what a menace the Peiping regime is. They respect and fear Russia but they refuse to see what Communism has done to China. Like many Americans a few years ago, they think of their neighbor across the Yellow Sea as "more Chinese than Communist." And they are used to dealing with old-fashioned China. As Shigeru Yoshida, a former premier, put it: "We don't have to be afraid. After all, the Chinese never invaded us. We always invaded them."

This refusal to recognize how revolution has transformed China into a dynamic force is politically convenient for the Japanese. By insisting they are not menaced by China, they prepare the logic for two popular policies: development of trade with the Communist Chinese, and refusal to set about the costly business of rearming, as the United States would like.

Japan wants to get its foot in the Chinese commercial door. Its ultimate economic interest is to gain access to Manchuria's coal and iron and to resume its large prewar exports of manufactured goods. Already Japanese statesmen are assuring us that this is the only way for their impoverished country to get back upon its feet sufficiently to meet the cost of rearming. They say: "You expect us to pay reparations to your World War allies. You also want us to pay off our postwar relief debt to you. We simply cannot afford to do this and to rearm as well unless we improve our economic position by developing trade with Communist China."

From our point of view, a strong Japan is as important to Asia as a strong West Germany is to Europe. But it is plain we will have as much difficulty rearming our former enemy in the East as we originally encountered in rearming our former enemy in the West. The Japanese see no need to pay more for security if they can get it cheaper from us. And they are not afraid of China.

Japan is not only our most important Asian ally, but also our second greatest international market. Commerce with us is vital to Japanese traders. Diplomacy must ultimately respond to their requirements. Since Tokyo lost both overseas empire and East Asiatic economic sphere, it has depended for sustenance upon the United States. Dollars earned by exports to us are necessary to purchase the raw materials required by Japanese factories: coal, iron, cotton, and petroleum. And our farmers find in Japan their largest single outlet.

The Japanese hope to expand sales in America. Nevertheless, prospects are limited. Our manufacturers dislike the thought of further competitive incursions. Therefore, Tokyo scans the rest of the world for other opportunities. However, in Western Europe it sees a restrictive common market—sponsored by us. And in the Commonwealth, not only Britain but Australia, New Zealand, and even India refuse to accord equal treatment.

In Asia, Japan is hampered by two factors. There is a heritage of resentment left in lands like Indonesia and the Philippines by Tokyo's imperial armies. And on the mainland we have forced the Japanese to participate in our economic blockade against the Communist bloc. While still patient under these circumstances, it is to the mainland and, above all, to China that their industrialists ultimately look. We tell them this is a different China; that it makes its own textiles and needs its own iron and coal. But the Japanese remember prewar days when Manchuria fed their hungry furnaces. Their businessmen have been scouring the continent. They return with optimistic views, and this is reflected in Tokyo's policy aspirations.

Japan would like to tidy up the complex Chinese picture. It favors a "two China" solution which would guarantee Formosan independence while recognizing Peiping. It hopes mercantile restrictions on the Communist bloc will gradually wither away. It even desires a reunited neutralized Korea.

Our own diplomacy must plan for possible contingencies. Peiping has promised massive trade if Japan denounces its security treaty with us. China pledges aid in restoring sovereignty over American-occupied Okinawa. This impresses Japan's opposition Socialists. Right now they are weak and their prospects poor. But any economic crisis might easily catapult them into office.

Our government should aid Japan in its continual search for commerce. Far more difficult is the territorial question. On paper we promise to give back the Bonin and Ryukyu islands, including Okinawa. But the Pentagon refuses even to permit expelled Japanese to return to the Bonins or to allow Tokyo control of education or civil administration in the Ryukyus. It argues: "Why risk trouble where there is none now?" For the short range this looks practical. But someday Okinawa will become the Cyprus of anticolonialist America.

The Pentagon deems it essential that we retain absolute control of Okinawa for an indeterminate period because of the Sino-Soviet threat. Obviously, with the trend of weapons development, it is fated to become a missile ramp. This situation has been strategically beneficial not only to ourselves but to the Japanese and to Chiang on Formosa. The advantage of our umbrella for Tokyo is that its territory can be protected by us at minimal cost through threats of retaliation from Okinawa. But this poisons our friendship with the Japanese. Whether we remain in Okinawa *de facto* or *de jure,* our presence implies a form of that colonialism which we condemn in others. Britain claimed Cyprus as a strategic base. To the simple-minded Japanese this argument does not differ from our pretensions to Okinawa.

The Pentagon has been able to prevail over the State Department in this aspect of Oriental policy making. In fact, so much has the Pentagon prevailed that, as part of our Far Eastern strategic posture, we promised Chiang in 1954 not to diminish our Okinawa garrison without consulting him first. In exchange he agreed not to invade the Chinese mainland without consulting us.

This, George Yeh, then Chiang's foreign minister, said to me was the inner meaning of the Yeh-Dulles letters that accompanied our formal treaty with Formosa five years ago. Thus, in an ultimate sense, Chiang has implied veto power over our Japanese relationships, for the latter hinge upon how we dispose of Okinawa.

There is only one course for us to prevent a dangerous impasse from developing. That is to negotiate new security arrangements with Tokyo, complementing those that already exist, to insure sufficient retaliatory bases in Japan. Then we should relinquish political control over the Ryukyus and the Bonins, a preserve of the United States Navy.

We cannot permit our curious understanding with Chiang to interfere with such arrangements. If we allow the present Okinawa situation to develop, it will develop in only one way —that of Cyprus. We will find an increasing hostility among the islanders—as Britain encountered with the Cypriots. We will meet bitterness among the Japanese, as the British did in

Greece. And we will sacrifice any moral pretensions to champion anticolonialism.

The only other potential power in free Asia is democratic India, a massive but still chaotic nation. If Japan is the key to East Asia, India is the key to South Asia. United States foreign policy as applied in South Asia displays a disturbingly schizophrenic aspect. Our aspirations are clearly both benevolent and sound. But the methods by which we seek to achieve them are almost surely self-defeating.

Our fundamental objective is to seal off the Sino-Soviet bloc and prevent Communism from intruding southward. To bolster the underdeveloped countries affected, we are sponsoring a dual program. One phase is purely military. This endeavors to strengthen defensive capabilities of nations committed to the Western camp. Pakistan comes specifically within this category as a member both of SEATO and the Baghdad Pact. The other phase is economic. This endeavors to strengthen the social, agricultural, and industrial structure of all South Asian nations, neutral or otherwise, enabling them to resist subversive pressures. In this category we include not only our ally Pakistan but countries often irritatingly unsympathetic to our aspirations—India, Ceylon, Burma, Nepal, and Afghanistan. Of these, India is overwhelmingly the most important.

Even American officials most angered by Nehru's tendency to lecture us while excusing Communist transgressions and his own violation of those principles he preaches admit that the West has an immense stake in Indian democracy's success, for India is the only huge Asian nation that remains non-Communist.

A curious competitive coexistence obtains between New Delhi and Peiping. The Russians, recognizing the importance of this contest, are pouring vast material, technical, and financial aid into China. We, likewise, are investing a considerable amount in efforts to help Nehru's democratic revolution—

even though Washington tends to dislike his personality. If, during the coming generation, India can succeed in modernizing its antiquated plant, educating its illiterate masses, and becoming self-sufficient, the cause of freedom will have achieved a triumph. Eventual repercussions in other Asian nations, even ironbound China, might be endless.

However, the chances of Indian success in this competition with China are being hampered by an arms race with Pakistan. Part of India's budget is supported by our economic generosity. But another part is drained off by New Delhi's determination not to lag behind Karachi militarily. Pakistan's matériel comes from us. Both countries spend on defense infinitely more than they can afford. The amount in each case is probably over half the national income. Neither, within the foreseeable future, can become strong enough to stave off open Sino-Soviet aggression. But each is rapidly attaining a capability to cripple the other.

American policy of arming Pakistan helps indirectly to weaken disastrously the Indian economy. It has also provoked another neighboring land, Afghanistan, to make an unhealthy weapons deal with the U.S.S.R. on the assumption such equipment is required because of a frontier argument with the Pakistanis. Therefore, by our policy, we encourage a sterile military-spending race. None of the South Asian countries can afford this. And India's long-range planning, upon which we ultimately base such hopes, is going down the drain.

This situation allows Moscow two political choices. The Russians have already offered India vast credits. They may suggest still larger amounts in an effort to gain controlling leverage on India's economy. Or they may withdraw proposed help in the hope of stimulating collapse and possible disintegration of Asia's largest democratic nation.

By our well-intended policy of arming Pakistan, we are unwittingly helping to sabotage India's social revolution—upon which we bet so heavily. Clearly the time has come to think this through more carefully. Pakistan, as our ally, is surely entitled to be strong. But has not the moment already arrived to cut down military assistance to that country and help develop its disturbingly backward economy? Should we make such a decision, it is certain that India can be prevailed upon to reduce investment in unproductive weapons.

It would be shortsighted folly if, for the sake of strengthening our ally's limited fighting potential, we helped destroy Asia's most important non-Communist revolution—and, by so doing, lost Asia itself.

In finding a new foundation for our Asian policy we might well ponder these facts:

The Russians made it apparent in the Geneva summit talks that formal truce could be obtained for Europe only at the price of continued partition of Germany. Their immediate goal appears to be a collective security agreement between NATO and Communism's "Anti-NATO" with each of the two German governments participating. This still appears to be the true Soviet objective although it has been obscured by talk of "disengagement" and by Moscow's hints that it would be prepared to see a neutralized Germany reunited by direct negotiations between its Eastern and Western components. Chancellor Konrad Adenauer's regime detests this idea. So does the United States.

Later the Chinese Communists proposed a "collective peace" agreement in Asia. This bears rudimentary resemblance to Moscow's European scheme. But the Far Eastern situation has not yet frozen, as in Europe. Consequently, Peiping rejects for Asia the very *two-national* theory that Moscow hopes to apply in Europe. China is against two Vietnams, two Koreas, or two Chinas. It hopes its dynamism may yet conquer those countries by patient political subversion.

And if, for obvious reasons, Communism's global policy

seems compounded of dichotomy, so is our own. We refuse to consider a Communist proposal for a collective security arrangement in Europe because it is founded upon acceptance of two Germanys. But we also refuse to consider a similar arrangement in Asia because it does not accept the idea of two Chinas. The reasons for this apparent contradiction in logic are plain. Still, the result is anomaly.

As if this were not confusing enough, it is worth recalling that during the past decade Washington and Peiping have both shifted 180 degrees in policy on Formosa. Since the Cairo Conference in 1943, we contended the island was part of China. Now we would happily settle for its independence. But until 1949 Mao Tse-tung talked solely of a free Formosan republic. Only after Chiang Kai-shek fled there in 1949 did the Communists start claiming the island as Chinese territory. We are still poles apart on the issue, but we have moved to each other's poles.

Neither Washington nor Peiping can yet afford to abandon its present position. But someday there can be reassurance of Far Eastern peace along lines, believe it or not, inferentially suggested by Dulles. The price will inevitably be admission to the United Nations of the Chinese People's Republic. The Secretary of State wants both Chinas to observe the principle that "force shall not be used to achieve national ambitions." The U.N. Charter specifically outlaws force. Thus, by joining the United Nations, Peiping would assume moral obligations that did not technically apply when it started the Korean aggression.

One question that must arise when Peiping is eventually admitted to the U.N. is that of China's permanent Security Council seat, now held by Formosa. A solution that has been discussed is to award this to India—thereby avoiding the necessity of a Solomonic decision between two Chinas. The Indians are privately delighted with the thought. This is one reason they push so hard for Sino-American parleys.

China has replaced Soviet Russia as the greatest power in Asia. But the People's Republic remains a clay-footed colossus dependent upon outside aid. The U.S.S.R. alone has not been able to furnish this help without suffering serious strain. Will we ever want to ease the burden?

We cannot but rejoice to see our ideological enemies beset by massive problems. Yet the more we reduce tension with Peiping, the less it will be compelled to rely on Moscow. Is it our long-range hope to see two capitals of Communism—a Rome and a Constantinople—and to assume that inevitably schism will develop between them?

In the end, all our Asian policy revolves around one burning issue: China. Our intricate and unfortunately ineffective Eastern alliance structure is aimed at hemming in an ever-more-dynamic Oriental Communism. Our commercial relationships are governed by anti-Chinese strictures. Our economic attitudes are founded on the desire to support huge indigenous armies in such impoverished lands as Pakistan and South Korea.

We have compromised our moral attitude on colonialism and risk poisoning friendship with Japan because of a need to develop bases in territory not technically ours. We have frightened Asian neutrals and, above all, India by what has appeared to be unyielding support of avowed jingoes. We have worked out treaty links and a three-prong strategy that are inoperable. This is an unsound situation. And yet we fear to change it.

It would be common sense, not appeasement, to begin to adjust to facts. There is no sense in pell-mell, abrupt changes. But policy should now make it apparent what our ultimate intentions are. We still remain the strongest nation in the world. Such being the case, it is foolish even to appear to base policy for the globe's most populous continent on dreams of restoration of the past. And, in contemplating with sad sentiment a

newly dynamic Asia, we might well remember these words of
Edna St. Vincent Millay:

> No further from me than my hand
> Is China that I loved so well;
> Love does not help to understand
> The logic of the bursting shell.

Chapter 8

Where Policy Goes Wrong

The greatest asset of Soviet diplomacy since Stalin's death is that it has succeeded in giving an appearance of change. Its objectives may not swerve, but its methods are now subtle and successful.

"Change is the law of life," Secretary Dulles once said, "and that includes international life." Is it not time for us to ponder change in our foreign policy?

In approaching this problem we must define what we seek in world affairs. We know our aspirations are peaceable and our generosity is renowned. Why cannot everyone accept this at face value? There are perhaps several reasons.

At the heart of the matter rests confusion, even among those who govern us, concerning the nation's real desires. We have allowed our policy to become synonymous with anti-Communism. This forces us to sacrifice both sense and flexibility. Anti-Communism alone is no policy. Hitler discovered this.

Yet surely what we desire is clear enough. We want peace, but not at any price. We intend to protect our vital interests. We wish to prevent dissolution of free, friendly nations. We are ready to deal with all who support these aims. And we go wrong when we fail to concentrate upon such plain ideas.

Our enemy is no specific ideology—but all ideologies tied to aggression. It is that simple. Unfortunately, however, our leaders too often describe our intentions in meaningless generalities designed to soothe the voter. They resemble those statesmen described by a Chinese sage, Lao-tzu, who "just made everything pleased with itself while they maintained their poise in the incommensurable and wandered in the nonexistent."

Such linguistic ritual does not defeat a messiah. And, to some of this earth's discouraged and dispirited peoples, Communism remains a messianic faith. All nations do not regard the fat-dripping comfort of our life as a historical acme. Should we not remember that other satisfied regimes have crumpled in the past? We must never forget that self-deception can lead to political dementia.

Nevertheless, we are given to self-deception. We deceived ourselves about our technical superiority over Russia. We continue to deceive ourselves about reality in China. We even deceive ourselves about ourselves. We are pleased with our accomplishments. Therefore, we assume our methods are suitable to everyone. American democracy has, on the whole, worked well for us. But other peoples of different heritage and circumstance would not know what to do with it.

Our own democracy is patently imperfect. Had we been more aware of this and postured less righteously abroad, we need not have been so embarrassed by the shame of Little Rock. In foreign affairs humility can play a role. Lao-tzu counseled: "Discard righteousness and the people will regain the love of their fellows."

Clearly, we must cease diplomatic sermonizing. This applies to preachments by our leaders on the rights and wrongs of neutralism, on national versus international Communism, on some nations' colonialism and our own anticolonialism—as expressed in Okinawa. There is sense in modesty. Let us no longer delude ourselves about how good we are. Dulles says: "We do not assume the right to meddle or be the arbiter of other peoples' affairs." Admittedly the cause was just, but what were we doing in Guatemala or in Italy's 1948 elections?

If we wish to scrutinize the logic of diplomacy, let us examine our own contradictions. We preach democracy to states which cannot apply it, and simultaneously we support dictators. Many Africans and Asians are unsuited for either our politics or our economics. America's system is tailored for a relatively underpopulated nation rich in resources. Yet we sponsor it in lands where it might wreck the beneficiaries. And, with no sense of embarrassment, we ally ourselves with Franco, Salazar, Batista, Field Marshal Sarit, and the slave-owning King Saud.

This anomaly would appear less strange were we to stop our lecturing. Policy is a matter of national self-interest. France's "Most Christian" king once banded with the Sultan against a pope. When we fought beside Russia, we did not fool ourselves about its dogma.

Too often reality is obscured by wishful thinking. We confound diplomatic recognition with political approval. The Baltic states vanished two decades ago; but we still recognize them. We continue to act as if Chiang Kai-shek speaks for all China, not Formosa.

We insist that Communism is repugnant to religious persons. Yet it manages to penetrate Islam. We assume, so Dulles says, that Communism will become more liberal. This is contrary to the advice of Milovan Djilas, now in a Communist prison. How often do we build on false assumptions?

As I have written earlier, a nation's foreign policy is judged not only in terms of content but of style. The style of our diplomacy often appears unnecessarily awkward. We are given to hasty judgments and crash programs which too frequently are a consequence of insufficient foresight.

Widely advertised journeys by our statesmen can lead to rebuffs affecting our prestige. For example, there was simply no point in rushing George Allen to Cairo after Nasser made his 1955 arms deal with the Soviet bloc. Nothing was accomplished but loss of face.

It is distressing how little co-ordination there appears to be in some statements and actions of our leaders. Secretary Dulles's abrupt backing and filling on the Aswan Dam is a classic of ineptitude. One wonders why certain public declarations are necessary at all.

In 1956 President Eisenhower spoke sympathetically of other countries' neutralism. Almost immediately his words were corrected by Dulles. Vice-President Nixon then sought to "clarify" the contradiction. And Herbert Hoover, whose name is still renowned, compounded the tumult by denouncing Communism, socialism, and neutralism as, all three, "evil ideas."

Less hectoring, fewer voyages of discovery, and more conventional diplomacy through quiet ambassadorial channels would clearly seem desirable. But here again we face a weakness created needlessly by ourselves. This is the debilitation of our Foreign Service.

During the past few years, as a consequence of internal political pressures, our government cruelly dismissed some of its ablest envoys. Others were demoted in importance, and in circumstances not yet generally known. And, as is our foolish tradition, we have named to missions abroad men whose only qualifications were wealth or political fidelity.

This is nonsensical behavior for a superpower so dependent upon its international position. It is ridiculous to make either fortune or party fealty a condition for representing us. It is an anachronism that personal prosperity remains a *sine qua non* for some of our most vital embassies. No man of moderate means can undertake to act as envoy for our rich republic in London, Paris, or Rome. In choosing their representatives to us, other lands are in no sense so inhibited.

Five years ago, the State Department earnestly advised:

"The work of diplomacy requires intimate knowledge of the political customs, governmental forms and cultural patterns of people who work, think and worship in a manner quite different from our own. Understanding in these complex matters cannot be acquired overnight. It must be the product, not alone of specialized training, but of continuous and disciplined growth through experience, study, social contact and perceptive observation. Diplomacy has become serious, urgent and arduous business."

This is indeed an accurate statement. But was the answer suitably to be discerned in Mr. Gluck, our recent envoy to Ceylon? The Eisenhower administration, like almost every other administration which preceded it, has allowed Gresham's law to apply to our diplomatists. Under Gresham's law bad money drives out good. Is Gluck a worthy substitute for Kennan?

Ability and experience should be an ambassador's only qualifications. Adequate salaries and allowances must therefore be squeezed out of Congress if we are to be represented with maximum efficiency. Business success and political faith do not necessarily make a Talleyrand.

The hysteria of McCarthyism has fortunately faded. But its scars remain perceptible in some of our diplomatic missions. That boldness and independence of thought which marked the attitude of certain of our ablest Oriental specialists has almost vanished since the great China purge.

It is astounding how one can yet find servants of the State Department who, while knowing better, dare but reiterate the gospel as originally laid down by Walter Robertson: that Mao is tottering and Chiang will someday, willy-nilly, go back to Peiping. Hardly anyone in Asia now believes this.

We must base policy upon reality. And accurate reporting is a requisite for sound analysis. But all too often one has an eerie feeling that McCarthy's recent Know-Nothing movement still taints our international judgments.

Our policy will never have the mature style it merits until all its agents are appointed solely for ability and ordered to speak the uninhibited truth. Then we can turn more confidently to conventional channels for negotiation—like the Warsaw talks with China or the secret Trieste parleys. We must resume this pattern while reducing public pronouncements to a considered and co-ordinated minimum. Only thus will our prestige regain the gravity that is its due.

Farsightedness is essential to a successful foreign policy. But Washington has all too often shown capacity for diplomatic myopia. Our State Department has sometimes been shrewd in its forecasts and skillful in its negotiations. However, the picture contains too many holes. We fought World War II without a strategy for the ensuing peace. We sent an expedition to Lebanon with no thought of future policy there —except possibly to invade Iraq, which we did not do. Our soldiers were left to sit on their bayonets, about the only purpose that instrument is unsuited for.

Dulles's Policy Planning Staff had no advance position paper assessing probable effects if Egypt nationalized Suez. Nevertheless, was not such a step a likely consequence of our own policy? We strongly urged Britain to quit the canal zone. Then we publicly affronted the emotional Nasser on the issue of his pet Aswan Dam.

We had no program worked out ahead defining our attitude in case of uprising among the Soviet satellites. There had already been the early warning of East Germany's revolt. At least by inference we encouraged the desperate Hungarians. But we were caught without a plan of action.

Dulles showed little prevision when he needlessly intruded into the functions of our press and banned reporters from China. This cost us prestige in the Orient and eventually made us Peiping's laughingstock.

Prior to sputnik's launching, we apparently gave scant consideration to its conceivable propaganda and diplomatic repercussions. Yet we knew for at least two years that Moscow was working on this project. We ourselves had speculated that such a device, made in America, might have effects in apparently unrelated fields.

Planning inadequacies are no Republican copyright. In 1947 the Truman administration clearly helped French moderates gain an election victory over De Gaulle. Had we considered the possibility that this might saddle France with an unworkable constitution?

For years the Democrats ignored the Indochina puzzle. Later Washington spurned British ideas for a Southeast Asia alliance. This was finally invented by ourselves only after the area SEATO protects had been well penetrated.

Until Arab revolts spread across Africa's northern border, we seemed to forget that continent existed. Only in 1958 did we separate supervision of our African interests from those in South Asia and the Middle East. We have not yet begun to calculate an attitude toward the peoples of Soviet Central Asia—a region bound someday to trouble Moscow with its nationalism.

We never considered a "two Chinas" formula when there was still time to impress such a settlement on Taipei and Peiping. We seem to be switching now to the concept that Chiang Kai-shek and his successors will at least rule in Formosa. But the majority of Formosans are unenthusiastic. And Chiang continues, at least inferentially, to claim the mainland.

Problems elsewhere have been made an adjunct to the problems of Taipei, which receives disproportionate aid from us. To obtain Chiang's pledge not to invade the Asiatic continent without consulting Washington, we promised not to diminish our Okinawa garrison without consulting him. Thus he has veto power over our ultimate relationships with Japan.

We assume a new Peiping aggression will be met by what Dulles calls "three-prong strategy"—counterattacks from

SEATO, Formosa, and South Korea. But other SEATO powers have advised us they will not necessarily join in riposte to attacks on Chiang or Syngman Rhee. What would be the attitude of Japan, where we have bases?

Our policy has been afflicted by pactomania. NATO is a viable coalition, built upon the Marshall Plan's sound economic structure. Our Latin-American commitments developed logically from the Monroe Doctrine's legacy. But some of our Middle Eastern and Far Eastern pacts are flabby. It took no genial prescience to foresee that the Northern Tier alliance we promoted would irk India unnecessarily and inspire closer ties among Moscow, Cairo, and Damascus. This is what occurred. And now Baghdad, which gave the pact its name, cold shoulders it.

After the first sputnik, we sought to invigorate NATO with a grand meeting of heads of government. Nevertheless, during six years, we failed to assign to the alliance Council another superambassador of Harriman's stature or to keep our envoy sufficiently briefed on all our policy intentions.

Faulty planning helped us into an impasse. We will not be able to resolve the China problem or to pacify the Middle East until we sit down and bargain with the Communists. Mao Tse-tung rules in China. Russia is in the Middle East—even though the Eisenhower Doctrine is supposed to keep it out. The barn door was closed on the wrong side of the horse.

Must we negotiate basic settlements with Moscow, the value of whose agreements is so dubious? It is disagreeable to contemplate the possibility. But the power of weapons now available to both blocs is out of balance with the objectives for which they might be used.

Does this not impel diplomacy to look for the best obtainable compromise? In some areas, at least, we have strayed to an apparent dead end from which neither of our favorite policy slogans, containment or liberation, can extricate us.

Under two postwar administrations, our foreign policy has

been heavily influenced by military considerations. Our aid program is, for obvious reasons, overweighted in favor of defense and defense support. The Pentagon has had immense say in many diplomatic decisions. One consequence is the spread of military dictatorships imposed by armies we build up.

It is time to review this situation in terms of both Europe and Asia. Is our course economic and prudent? Has it adjusted sufficiently to a changing world situation?

As far as Europe is concerned, there is reason for optimism. The Soviet bloc has not yet solved its satellite relationships, and, on our side of the ideological border, NATO shows enough vitality to undergo needed alterations. The alliance was conceived when present instruments of war were hardly to be imagined. And we alone had a large stockpile of nuclear weapons and superior means of delivering them. It was designed to deter attack from the East or to check it long enough for massive retaliation to come into play. The Russians have managed to right the atomic balance while maintaining preponderance in conventional forces. Therefore, our allies worry about what kind of protection we can afford them. Clearly, if they are to retain faith in us, we must make available to their armies missiles and new explosives. And clearly this will at least in part be done.

But in Asia the cold war presents more complex aspects. In the area between the Middle and Far East we made two evident miscalculations. We underestimated Kremlin ability to help underdeveloped nations. And we overstressed our own military aid.

Dulles reckoned, when Russia began its offers of foreign assistance, that Moscow was capable only of what he called "one-shot" programs. He thought the constant drain of China, the U.S.S.R.'s immense military budget, and its evident economic difficulties would prevent serious loans or grants to others. He seems to have misjudged the circumstances. Soviet funds are flowing to Afghanistan, India, Egypt-Syria, Iraq, Burma, and Indonesia, and have been dangled elsewhere.

Asia and Africa are convinced of the Marxist precept that nonindustrialized countries are doomed to relative degeneracy. They look abroad for boosts into the machine age. But thanks to a Pentagon bias in American policy decisions, most of the dollars we have sent have gone for unproductive purposes. Of the 150 billion dollars we disbursed overseas during recent years, the greater proportion was allocated for direct or indirect defense. We have helped build armies incapable of fighting modern war upon economies incapable of supporting such establishments. This has not greatly helped the beneficiaries. Their populations are less interested in guns than in butter, more concerned with freeing their children from want than they are with ideology.

Furthermore, to accomplish our desires, we have been forced by conditions to work from the top down. We channel our contributions through existing and often corrupt governments with the result that popular share in any benefits is restricted. To make our programs work, we must maintain a frequently unsatisfactory, if not impossible, *status quo*. The Communists, who oppose us, work from the bottom up, capturing popular discontent with prevailing administration. And they are able sometimes to paint us as those responsible for keeping in power despots who impoverish the people. How we can meet this challenge is difficult to say. But we must develop more pliancy in our aid and more support among the masses who should ultimately get it.

Moscow's subtle new regime benefits by contrast with the recent rigidity of Stalin. But we seem too inflexible. Our Asian alliances have been no great success. The Northern Tier we sponsored failed to keep Soviet influence from the Middle East. The Eisenhower Doctrine is unfashionable in that area. We can never hope to align the Arab states in any broad anti-Russian military pact. It is questionable whether such was ever worth attempting. Indeed, we must work to prevent precisely the opposite from occurring—a Moscow-sponsored anti-Western pact. SEATO is militarily weaker now than when it was invented, thanks to French troop withdrawals from Indochina and British force cuts. It is backstopped by our own ANZUS arrangement with Australia and New Zealand and by ANZAM, an entente between the latter lands and formerly British Malaya. ANZAM is now virtually non-existent. The new Malayan government claims never even to have heard of it.

It is not easy to stiffen the free world in the East. But the emphasis of our approach must shift. Economic assistance there is more important than military gear. Liberty must be worth something before a people is prepared to fight for it.

And we have yet to capture the imagination of newly independent masses. Communism, which they do not comprehend, is not the major threat for many of them. The major threat is fear of slipping backward into misery. Rifles cannot win that battle.

In a democracy, foreign policy must be based upon popular support. But emotional politics often obscures reason and national interest before public opinion has matured. The United States has suffered from this since the days of Woodrow Wilson. Wilson's clumsiness in facing political reality produced an isolationism opposite to the internationalist course he favored.

Since we abandoned President Pierce's formula for dealing with governments regardless of ideology, the question of diplomatic recognition has been the subject of much agitation. The issue of exchanging ambassadors with Soviet Russia or Franco Spain became a political football rather than a matter of diplomatic wisdom. This is even truer with China.

America has a long tradition of affection for the Chinese. This affection, magnified during World War II, helped subject our national attitude to unusual stresses. Our sensible approach after Mao Tse-tung's revolution was to "let the dust settle" before elaborating policy. But first party politics, then the Korean war made impossible the necessary period of calm. Only now is any dust settling. Without admitting it, we have "leashed" Chiang Kai-shek, although for some years we still proclaimed the opposite to be the case.

When Moscow provoked the Korean aggression, it succeeded in further isolating China from us. Peiping had thenceforth to rely upon the Kremlin for its very existence. This situation cannot hastily be altered. Upon its continuation we have constructed our concomitant policies in the East.

Yet it is increasingly apparent Chiang will never be able to return. Even in the unlikely case of major revolt against Peiping, he would hardly be accepted as a "new" sign of change. The Chinese respect success—and Chiang failed badly. In Polish terms what they want is a "Gomulka," not a "General Anders."

Mao's administration at first did well—with great brutality. It established an unprecedented period of internal peace. The Korean war did not greatly affect the national economy. The regime could look back upon restored order, the beginning of industrialization, and one excellent crop year.

The Russians played a smart game. Their technicians were briefed on what they could and could not do. While giving much technical aid, they remained in the background. Moscow was careful not to force its ideology down Chinese gullets. Peiping, while maintaining close governmental relationships, makes its own doctrinal interpretations. Thanks to Soviet tact, nothing like the Yugoslav heresy developed.

Nevertheless, difficulties have arisen. Agriculture fared badly in 1956. People began to realize upon what a weak foundation the economy was built. Without food it became impossible to maintain distribution of machinery and commodities. Industrialization slowed down while pressure of population, increasing at the rate of eighteen million a year, necessitated manufacture of even more consumers' goods.

Although crops have improved, discontent has grown again in China. Mao's effort to establish the nation's farming basis on a huge, inhuman factory system is bound to produce an almost uncontrollable fury among the helpless peasants. Where does this situation leave us?

We still support Chiang as titular claimant to all China and legitimate ruler in Formosa. But, despite mainland unhappiness, he is almost surely not destined to go back. And the majority of Formosans, who have no mainland connections, resent his rule.

Peiping insists it can negotiate a private solution on Formosa. It has the island well infiltrated. Many spies with fancy communications have been unveiled. Subversive approaches have been made at high levels. When Chiang dies, is it not possible his successors might seek an accommodation?

We hope to keep Formosa from Communist domination and within our Pacific defense chain. Japan and the Philippines back us in this approach, which, someday, must be the subject of bartering. There is reason to suspect Peiping would accept any ultimate solution leading toward diplomatic recognition and admission to the U.N., even admitting Formosan independence—as Formosa, not another "China."

We have made recognition the subject of negotiation and we are in a position to grant it, for a satisfactory *quid pro quo,* without making things easier for China by giving economic aid. Such a *quid pro quo* should be the goal of present diplomacy, sought in quiet caution.

There is little hope of helping the Chinese to find their own Gomulka while keeping them in isolation. And surely the Russians are delighted with our present policy of exclusion, which allows them to speak for Mao.

It is time for us to consider more flexible approaches designed to meet the realities of the world. But this cannot be attempted too hurriedly. Any pell-mell rush would stagger our Asian friends.

What we first need is return to pondered realism: another attempt to let dust settle amid the revolutionary storm. But we must keep that same dust out of our own eyes so we can observe the facts.

Foreign policy is neither abstract art nor science. Its aims and methods must continually adjust to changing world conditions. This is especially true in a democracy where each administration is bound by commitments of its predecessors and, in turn, obligates its own successors. Our attitude toward the new China began in 1949 when Communism seized the mainland, and developed after 1950 during the Korean war. The much-debated Northern Tier, south of Russia, was conceived before the Eisenhower government. Wherever our German policy may ultimately lead, its course was fixed under President Truman. Neither the mistakes nor successes of United States diplomacy are the sole property of either political party. With this in mind we may examine where our expressed aspirations can lead.

In China the outlook is perplexing. We hope someday to divide the Sino-Soviet alliance. Yet we do everything possible to strengthen it. We thrust Peiping into Moscow's arms and thus vitiate chances of heresy developing within the largest Communist state. Simultaneously, our national defense demands that Formosa be kept separate from the Marxist mainland. We work to insure that the island's government will remain in the hands of *émigrés* brought over by Chiang Kai-shek. But they represent only 20 per cent of the total population. And the majority has little interest in China. Peiping desires to negotiate an eventual private settlement with the mainland refugees. When Chiang dies, what is to prevent his

successors from arranging this? If that happens, we will have
lost not only China but Formosa. Yet our own policy points
to that dangerous possibility.

In Germany our attitude makes sense only if Washington is
in no hurry to unify that country. It is clear that while the
remilitarized West remains in NATO, Moscow will never
agree to reunification. Perhaps we really do not place a high
priority upon joining the partitioned land and, therefore, ad-
vocate impossible preconditions. France and Britain favor this
approach. If such is our view also, present policy is sound. But
if we wish to unfreeze the European ice jam, it is not sound.
Maybe this is a matter of timing. When Bonn's rearming is
more advanced, conceivably our attitude may change. However, when that time comes, the Federal Republic will be in
a more powerful position to disregard our own desires and
act as free agent in negotiations with the Kremlin. Possibly
before that moment we will have to ponder more actively the
idea of "disengagement" and a neutral zone in Europe's heart.
Is this the purpose of the Kremlin's latest Berlin ploy?

In South Asia, the Northern Tier lost us more than it ever
gained. It shoved Afghanistan northward toward Russia by
favoring hostile Pakistan. For similar reasons, it infuriated
India, the only major power in free Asia. The SEATO alliance was developed far too late, thanks to our own obduracy
when London and Paris first desired it. It succeeded in checking Communism's military advance, but Moscow's world tactics have altered. Internal subversion is now the mode, as seen
in Laos, an area protected by the pact. Since the regional
danger is increasingly political, we must help remold the coalition's framework and philosophy.

In the Middle East, the Eisenhower Doctrine proved unworkable. We have secured no mass support among the Arabs.
Circumstances induced us to back outdated regimes and maintain an untenable *status quo*. We have not managed to settle
the perhaps insoluble puzzle of Israel inherited from Tru-

man's rash and emotional program. But we did go out of our way to irk Arab nationalists.

We helped produce the background that prompted Britain and France to embark on their disastrous Suez venture. Then we pulled the rug out from under them. Meanwhile, we neither support nor isolate Nasser. He therefore toys with us, flirts with Russia, and boasts of this to Pan-Arabia.

We permit foreseeable crises to fester and become cancerous. Cyprus is one example; Algeria another. A world power like the United States cannot be blind to others' problems. But all too often our policy specializes in dealing with emergencies we refused to foresee in advance, postponing compromise solutions when they were possible, and preparing empirical responses too late.

Everything in life contains the seeds of its own destruction. This is true, as Marx saw, of capitalism. It is also true of Communism. All systems must adjust themselves continually in order to survive. Rigidity is doomed. By the time any truly perceptive genius can interpret history's constantly changing laws, those laws again have changed.

Lenin wrote *Imperialism, the Final Stage of Capitalism.* We hope to write someday "Imperialism, the Final Stage of Communism." Neither title yet applies. And before the last chapter of one or the other treatise becomes valid, we must prepare for an enduring contest. In this we can never afford to abandon our basic principles. But we cannot maintain them practicably unless, in the process, we survive. This is the task of our foreign policy.

Index

249